AN OFFERING OF UNCLES

An Offering of Uncles

The Priesthood of Adam
and
the Shape of the World

ROBERT FARRAR CAPON

CROSSROAD · NEW YORK

1982
The Crossroad Publishing Company
575 Lexington Avenue, New York, N.Y. 10022

Printed in the United States of America

Library of Congress Catalog Card Number: 81-70386

ISBN: 0-8245-0422-4

Contents

AN OFFERING OF UNCLES

I Prologue

AUCTOR: Well.

LECTOR: Well, what?

AUCTOR: Well, here we are.

LECTOR: But this is preposterous. An author is supposed to begin more surefootedly.

AUCTOR: Ah, but beginning is not that easy.

LECTOR: If you find it such a problem, why do you insist upon authoring?

AUCTOR: Because I have something to say.

LECTOR: Thank heaven for that. What is it?

AUCTOR: If I could tell you, I would have said it already.

LECTOR: Oh. And I suppose that since you have not said it, you cannot tell me?

AUCTOR: Precisely.

LECTOR: My congratulations. Your book is a model of brevity.

AUCTOR: Not quite. We are not yet ready to talk about a book, only a beginning. And my beginning is a model, not of brevity, but of honesty. The start of a book, you see, can be written either before or after the book itself. If before, it will be an honest but shakily written piece of business during which the author struggles to get his feet under him, and from which he escapes the first chance he gets. If afterward, it will be a piece of Fine Writing in which he ticks off briefly and with utterly fake aplomb all the things he has spent months trying to keep himself glued together long enough to say. In the first case it is a beginning, but not worth reading, and in the second it is readable, but no beginning. There is, therefore, no way to begin a book both honestly and successfully.

LECTOR: But that is obviously false. Many books begin well.

AUCTOR: You fail to distinguish. Books may begin well; authors do not. When an author sets out, he is only vaguely in possession of what he wants to say. He knows as much about his unwritten book as an architect knows about an unbuilt house: only, for example, how many rooms he wants, and whether the kitchen is to be central or auxiliary. The true work of composition must be done, hit or miss, from the ground up; to attempt it from the porch in will produce a monstrosity. The real beginning of a book, therefore, is always carefully suppressed. Not to do so would be an editorial sin comparable to leaving an excavation in front of a finished house.

LECTOR: I hope your editor has a firm grasp of all this. When will you ever begin?

AUCTOR: I already did. Two pages ago.

LECTOR: That is absurd. Give me something more definite, or I shall walk out.

AUCTOR: It is your privilege. These things take time. Would you be kind enough to ask me what I do for a living?

LECTOR: Very well, but it is my last exchange. What do you do for a living?

AUCTOR: I am a clergyman.

LECTOR: Is that all?

AUCTOR: No. I will make you a confession.

LECTOR: Good grief! Not one of those . . .

AUCTOR: Quiet! You have already had one exchange over your quota. You must listen or leave.

᭟

I have a recurrent fantasy. The characters in it sometimes change, but the metaphysical substance is always the same. It began a few years ago when my wife looked up from her mending to remark that, for a man in my profession, it would be more seemly if something other than the seat of my pants wore out first. The comment, I felt, had an edge to it. She knew perfectly well that I said my prayers standing, since I invariably fall asleep when I kneel. I found myself taking umbrage. Perhaps I felt guilty at not being heroic enough to kneel without leaning on a chair, or perhaps I was just parrying; but, at any rate, I gave her a short disquisition on the sedentary age we live in, and I ended with the comment that she did ill to complain—that in all

probability every housewife in America was engaged in a
ceaseless and noble struggle to close the wounds that civilization was inflicting upon our trousers.

It was the thought of that transcontinental concert of
trouser seats being worn away that led to the metaphysical
dimension. From the attrition of the pants it was only a
step to the attrition of the men inside the pants. I would
look at people I knew with the strange feeling that, through
the seats of their pants, they themselves were being worn
away—a little bit every year—so that it was a race with
death to see if there would be anything left of them to
bury. I would wonder what could be done to stop the
attrition—whether, for example, we would, as a race, have
to give up sitting in the interest of self-preservation. But
then I saw that the avoidance of sitting wouldn't help at
all, because the wearing was not being caused by the places
people sat in, but by the fact that they were not sitting in
places at all: they were set on top of a slowly grinding
placelessness. Do you see what I mean? If the seats they
sat in were *places*, they would destroy only cloth; but
because they are *noplace*, they wear out people.

One of the characters in the fantasy may help to explain
it: The Man on the Thruway. I would see him driving
a late model car from Buffalo to Albany. The inside of it
was typically nowhere. It used to be that the driver's seat
of an automobile was a recognizable place: the control
room of a traveling machine. But no more. There are still
knobs and gauges, but they have fewer and fewer necessary
connections with the inside of the car as *someplace*. Half
of them operate devices that could be anywhere: radios,

cigarette lighters; the rest control a machine that practically drives itself. And the gauges. The old ammeters and manometers are gone. They have been supplanted by apocalyptic little lights which give the driver no useful information about the place he is in: they simply announce accomplished disasters. And the principal gauge of all, opulently central, tells him only the speed at which he is missing other places. He sits upon sleek vinyl covers, his feet touch deep carpet; acoustical ceilings cover him, music embraces him. It all whispers to him—tells him perhaps that he is a tiger or a king, but in no known forest, over no real kingdom. Nothing says where he is—and nothing can. He is noplace.

He passes signs: Syracuse, Schenectady; he passes mile posts: 276; 189. They mean nothing to him. Place is irrelevant; distances have become times. Albany is two more hours; food is fifteen minutes. He passes scenery: trees, lawns. But it, too, is nowhere—the same grass, endless from Buffalo to Albany. He looks ahead: What is that? It is a bridge; but what bridge, in what place, he does not know. He looks aside: What is this? It is a cloverleaf—anywhere, and, therefore, nowhere. It is all real; but it has ceased to *matter*. The placelessness grinds into his soul. He grows thinner.

He stops to eat, stepping from nowhere into nowhere. The thruway restaurant is another sacrament of his placelessness. The same broadloom stretches wall to wall; the same vinyl upholstery bears him up. Music floats mindlessly in the dead room. He orders. It is the same food he ate after Buffalo, served by the same waitress. He pays and leaves:

out past familiar trash cans full of french fry bags and milkshake containers. The same flies buzz over them in the heat. He struggles to find his car, tries several doors until he finds one to fit his key, and drops with relief into nowhere again. He feels thinner still, but he is headed home.

He races against the nothingness that wears him away. Home at least may save him, build him, stop the attrition. A singular wife, a peculiar brood, local sandwiches, personal garbage. Places, things; fragments to shore against his ruin, props to lift him from the grindstone. He sits again and eats, and he begins ever so slightly to thicken. Unique and private voices speak to him, discrete and personal hands touch him. He struggles to place himself, to become some*thing*, some*where*. But the pain is too great. The voices make demands, and the hands will not be controlled. The grinding was easier to bear. He goes to his living room to relax.

Broadloom once more enfolds him; the vinyl enters into his soul. He sits again in noplace, and the last thin part of him wears down forever. He turns the knobs of the television. Sound swells from the dark oblong frame, the picture flickers on, and in the unechoing room he watches —and sleeps. Late at night his wife comes to switch off the set, but it is too late: Nowhere has done its work. The picture narrows to a point, burns for an instant, and disappears into the window on the void. In the chair are his clothes: worn trousers, worn shoes. Good enough with a little mending for his funeral; but the man himself is gone.

Nevertheless, at the end of the fantasy, I go through the motions of burying him—closed coffin to hide the tragedy. The funeral parlor proclaims his placelessness: broadloom and vinyl are his last country; men without faces bear him out. We drive down placeless roads to a cemetery laid with the grasses of the thruway. The grave is dug and waiting, but the coffin is lowered only slightly; it sways gently in the straps. The words are said, the mourners leave, and on a treeless plain he hangs forever in the air.

Men who have lived nowhere are buried nowhere.

No monument shall mark his head; no local roots clutch his breast.

Richmond and Kew have not undone him; Syracuse and Albany have not destroyed him.

No place wore him away, and nowhere receives him at last.

He shall return no more to his house; neither shall his place know him any more.

II The Marsh Reed

LECTOR: Well!
AUCTOR: Well, what?
LECTOR: Well—I never expected *that*.
AUCTOR: Neither did I. It is a chancy business.

ॐ

Proneness to fantasy is not the only effect of the sedentary life. A suburban parish priest, if he takes no steps to
resist the pattern of his days, will find himself car-cursed
and chairbound by the age of thirty-five. After eight years
of driving everywhere and walking nowhere, I had arrived,
short of wind and weak of limb, at the point of being
unable to take a flight of steps without thinking of heart
trouble. Exercise, of course, was the cure, but, as an unrepentant non-sportsman, my first concern was to find
some form of it that would keep me out of the clutches of
golf. It is, I suppose, the perfect clerical pastime, but it
is just not my dish. For one thing, it can get expensive;
for another, the exercise it provides is only intermittent,
and, for the truth, I am no good at it. I am a duffer, and
I am fit only for the duffer's part of the game. Once I had
faced that fact, the rest was easy. I simply took up walking.

I have been delighted with it. It is free. It takes only

reasonable amounts of time. It is always available. (It is
essential to walk in all weathers. The fair-weather walker
loses half the privileges of his sport: snow and rain, sun-
shine, fog, heat and cold—no exercise can match it for
variety.) And it works. I have no facts to support it, but
I have a theory that there must be a low incidence of heart
disease among letter carriers. At any rate, the pounding
heart is gone, the legs are usable again, and, doubtful blessing
though it may be, I am much longer winded than before.

But walking has turned out to have intellectual as well
as physical benefits. I am as much the victim of placelessness, as much the prisoner of canned environment as the
next fellow. It has, therefore, been a delightful and metaphysical surprise to be introduced to *place* again. I have, for
example, rediscovered what a hill is. The automobile is the
great leveler. It not only annihilates distances; it irons all
the prominences and eminences out of the world. I had
lived in Port Jefferson eight years as a parish priest, and I
thought I knew it as a place, thought I understood pretty
well how it gave itself out as *somewhere*. I was aware that
it was hilly, and that that, on Long Island, automatically
put it in select company: only the North Shore really rises
and falls; the rest is mostly unrelieved outwash plain. But
it wasn't until I walked up East Broadway for the first
time that I, as a person, met the village as a place. It is a
respectable hill. (The mark of a good hill, by the way, is
the absence of sidewalk on its upper reaches. That is its
letter patent of true prominence, the guarantee that only
real walkers ever go all the way up: children, the poor and
the possessed. From the point of view of the municipality,

such a motley crew as that can be left to walk in the gutter. Sidewalks are built for the sane.)

So I met my town on a hill, walking in the gutter for the last hundred yards, taking the land on its own terms, not mine. It was not an easy meeting—it never will be. It is physically impossible to take it at a normal walking pace and not be blown at the top. But it was a real meeting, and I am glad that the land can still leave me winded and refreshed.

It is another eight years now since I started walking; and up and down hills, past shacks and boat yards, along the waterfront and through shaded streets I have found place again. In any other age it would not be much of an achievement, but in this one it is worth a little self-congratulation. I am part of a town and I have not neglected the privileges of my membership.

Port Jefferson is just far enough away from New York City to have remained a small town, but it is also close enough to have felt the impact of the developers. More than half my parish lies outside the village proper. Sixteen years ago, the upland (and level) part of the countryside was rural: farms, woodlots and scrub oak. Since then the housing developments have come in. It isn't Levittown yet, but the smell is in the wind. The better looking ones, of course, have been left with a woodsy look about them, but even they are no place for a walker. The ones built on potato fields are just hopeless—great pieces of canned environment, dropped down in the middle of nowhere. It helps a little if they make the streets wind, but the repeating fronts of the five basic houses give it away: it is noplace.

Port Jefferson, on the other hand, is someplace, though, to tell the truth, it is not what it could be. It is untidy, distracted, and radically uncertain about just what place it is. But it is a place. There are a good many plans now to do it over, and, heaven knows, it needs it; but I don't look forward to the prospect. I don't trust the age to handle it properly.

The lower part of town, adjacent to the harbor, can be described with a little charity as a sprawling and indifferent sand lot: it was once a marsh, but it has been haphazardly filled in. Flowing across it, in a northeast path, is a creek which begins under the west hill and wanders toward the harbor. The creek is unavoidable and sempiternal; drainage demands it. Over the years, however, it has shrunk to the proportions of a glorified ditch. Along its length lies an assortment of junk: broken hulls, rusting metal—an anthology of seaside trash. I will trust any planner to see to it that it is cleaned up. But along its banks in places are great tall reeds with tasseled tops—the kind you can take home and make tiny whistle flutes of, if you spend a whole summer evening fooling with them. Do you think that the planners will leave those? What kind of odds will you give me that it will occur to any of them to make a park down there and encourage the reeds to grow the whole length of the creek? I wouldn't take your money. Not that the park wouldn't be worth it; it just will never happen. Or, if it does, they will pull up the reeds and plant marigolds. But I will give you two good reasons for it anyway.

The original name of Port Jefferson was Drown Meadow —a good, placey sort of name for a tidal swamp where men came to cut salt hay. In its wild state, it filled the space between wooded horseshoe hills and sank slowly under the edges of one of the best natural harbors on Long Island. Through most of its civilized history, however, it has been blessed (or cursed, if you don't like marine debris) with boat yards, gravel yards and oil yards. The architecture of the village itself runs a poor second to the distinguished disarray of its waterfront. But, through it all, the creek with its stands of reed has remained: a part of the city of things that was here before men built a town. For me, that is reason enough for a park and for a bank of reeds in perpetuity. But I do not plan to hold my breath till it arrives.

The other reason is personal. I give it to you as a treasured secret. Marsh reeds, when full grown, vary from five to ten feet in height, and the tassels on the ends of the good ones are thicker than squirrels' tails. The next time you walk past a bank of reeds, try something. Pick out the tallest one you can reach, and cut it off with your penknife as close to the ground as possible. Ostensibly, perhaps even to yourself, it will seem that you are cutting it down to carry home to your children. No one will take serious exception. But in the carrying of it, you will make a discovery. Keep a record of your reactions: *It is impossible simply to carry a marsh reed.* For how will you hold it? Level? Fine. But it is ten feet long, and plumed in the bargain. Are you seriously ready to march up the main street of town as a knight with lance lowered? Perhaps it would be less embarrassing to hold it vertically. Good. It rests gracefully in the crook of your arm. But now it is ten feet tall and makes you the bearer of a fantastic mace. What can you do to keep it from making a fool of you? To grasp it with one hand and use it in your walking only turns you from a king into an apostle; to try to make light of it by holding it upside down is to become a deacon carrying the inverted crozier at an archbishop's requiem. Do you see what you have discovered? There is no way of bearing the thing home without becoming an august and sacred figure—without being yourself carried back to Adam, the first King and Priest. So much so that most men will never finish the experiment: the reed, if cut at all, will never reach home. Humankind cannot stand very much reality: the strongest doses of it are invariably dismissed as silliness. But silly is from *selig*, and *selig* is blessed. If you ever want to walk your native ground in the sceptered fulness of the majesty of Adam, I commend the marsh reed to you. Whatever embarrassment it may cause you will be an *embarras des richesses*.

༗

My walking, therefore, has turned out to be money in my pocket—the recouping of an inheritance I had nearly been conned out of by a placeless age. But to walk through a village is not only to be restored to place. It is also to refresh the perception of the link between place and time, and so to come face to face with the fact of history. Place. Time. History. Ask any man whether he knows what they mean, and he will give you a confident Yes. He is sure he has grasped them for what they really are. But has he?

Hasn't there been, since Adam's fall, a sharp and recurrent temptation to miss the point of them completely—to substitute plausible little mental diagrams for them? And isn't this the age of the triumph of that temptation? We like to believe that we see ourselves as living in *places*, as acting in *time*, as the protagonists of real *history*. But we seldom get near the realities: it is the abstract substitutes, the mental counters, that our minds fasten upon. Listen.

For place we substitute *space*. Think of the creek with its bank of reeds. It is a place. If it is to be saved, to be lifted up, to be kept as a part of the real history of this village, it must be saved as what it is, *for itself*. But that is hardly the most likely thing that will happen to it. The overwhelming temptation of the planners will be to bury it in a conduit and to plant macadam on its grave. And why? Because they will never have looked at it as a *place*. For them it will have been only an abstraction, something contained within coordinates on a civil engineer's map—a nice empty *space* which, once its natural intractabilities have been tamed, can be converted into their favorite kind of packaged *locale*.

They have their reward. I have a theory that the membership of the architectural committee for hell is being recruited on Long Island, with the best jobs going to the people who have run creeks through conduits and built laundromats, muffler graveyards and motels along Route 25. I wish them no personal ill, but it would be against my principles to leave them without a curse: May ink run under their rulers forever, and their pencils break world without end.

And then there is time. And for time we substitute—
well, that takes a little explaining. Words are sometimes a
problem. *Time* in English is made to do far more work
than should reasonably be expected of any one word. In
Greek the labor of meaning is divided: there are two words
for time. For abstract time—for time as a diagram, a system
of coordinates—the Greeks had *chronos*: a solemn, un-
worldly notion they finally kicked upstairs and made a god.
We have it with us still in chronometers, chronology, and
chronicle. But for human time, for existential time—for
the time that is to *chronos* as place is to abstract space—they
had a word which, to the best of my knowledge, has not
come into English at all: *kairos*—season, *high time*, opportunity. The distinction is not airtight, but it is solid enough
to pass muster.

When I go for a walk in the morning, I notice the time
at which I leave the house: 8:45, for example. That is
chronos. Together with 9:10, it makes up the chronological
coordinates of my walk. It is time as it can be plotted and
drawn on a mental map. Once a man is trained to it, it is
a comforting notion. It is pleasant to know what time, what
chronos, it is, to be coordinated, to be on schedule. But
real time, high time—*kairos*, season opportunity, chance—
is not trapped within the coordinates of the clock. It does
not answer the minor question: What time is it? It goes
straight to the major one: What is it time *for*?

Ever since Einstein, the impression has gotten about
that somehow all our notions of time are inadequate. The
advances of mathematics and physics are said to have proved
that time is not absolute, but relative, and that, worse yet,

it can run at different rates for different people. For some years now the philosophical composure of the man in the street has periodically been sent sprawling by articles about what is called "the twin paradox." It seems to be a physical and mathematical certainty that if you sufficiently accelerate one of a pair of twins, you will start doing tricks with his time. When he gets back from his trip at something like the speed of light, he will find not only that he thought he had been gone less time than his brother reckoned, but that he *really had been*. Time would have gone slower for the traveller. His beard, if you please, would actually be shorter than his brother's.

To the common man, this is upsetting. He is used to conceiving of time as an absolute and unchanging continuum through which everyone passes at the eternally valid rate of sixty seconds per minute. But his consternation is based on a failure to distinguish *chronos* from *kairos*. *Chronos* never has been anything but relative. It seemed absolute only—precisely—because it was *cut off*, abstracted—because it had been turned into a god. *Chronos* seems constant only because all the clocks we can read—sun clocks, water clocks, escapement clocks, electric clocks, radioactive clocks, biological clocks, all clocks, down to the clock that makes my beard grow at the rate it does—are locked in the same relative velocity. It is a simple case of conspiracy. The answer to the question, "What time is it?", has always been a put-up job.

But *kairos* is different. With our customary skill, you see, we have gotten the whole thing exactly backwards. The man in the street thinks *chronos* is absolute and *kairos* is relative. He imagines that he will always be able to be sure what time it *is*, but will have to take potluck with what it is time *for*. As it turns out, however, what it is time *for* is the only thing that is not relative. Take the twin who left his brother at nearly the speed of light, but this time consider not the physical conditions of his being, but the man *himself*. Use your imagination. Call him Cain. Assume that his hasty departure was due to his having murdered his brother, and behold! You have broken the trap of time. You can let his *chronos*, his clock time, his biological time, do all the tricks it wants, but through all that relative *chronos* it will only be high time, *kairos*, for him to repent. And when, young, radiant and unrepentant, he climbs out of his capsule, the old unchanging law will be waiting for him. It will be a *kairos* for the assessment of his guilt and the payment of his debt. No matter what his *chronos* does —let him come back a thousand years too late for any living man to remember his crime—he will still come back in the same *kairos*: in time to hear the voice of his brother's blood crying from the ground.

Kairos, therefore, is the real thing, and *chronos* only a kind of game that a relative world is content to play. *Kairos* is the time of men, of events, of history; and *kairos*, not *chronos*, is the time I enter when I step out of my doorway at 8:45 o'clock. For, as I walk, *chronos* ceases to matter. What counts is not what time it is, but what it is time for. And there lies the true glory of walking.

The wind blows down the harbor and it is high time— a *kairos* rarer than inlanders think—for the smelling of the salt air. Or the hedges are in bud, and is a season, a *kairos*, for the chewing of privet leaves, for the relishing of green and bitter tastes. *Chronos* cannot find such things; he lives too high in the sky. These are events in the time of men. Their coordinates are not found on clocks, but in the conjunctions of the web of history, in the mutual confrontations of real beings.

If you want to prove all this to yourself, notice what happens the next time you go for a walk (a walk of refreshment, of course, not of necessity). First of all, you will, insofar as you give yourself to walking, cease to pay any serious attention to the clock. Your time spent in walking is time spent outside the coordinates of *chronos*. If you should happen to pass a clock during your walk, you will not know quite what to make of it. It will seem to have lost its connection with the time at which you set out. You know, of course, that it is in the same system—that even if, *per impossibile*, the lighting company took leave of its senses and started supplying 50-cycle current instead of 60, all the little synchronous motors in all the electric clocks would still keep perfect step and conspire to present *chronos* as the changeless god he is. But the clock in the middle of your walk is irrelevant because you have, by walking, immersed yourself in historic time, in *kairos*, in the time of due season and of singular conjunctions. You have entered a time in which *now* is not a dimensionless point at the end of the second hand, but a *kairos* as wide and as high as all history.

For *now* is when the gull sits on the piling and the world is still. And *now* is when he leaves, dropping lazily before he glides and rises. And *now* is when the sun goes for good behind the growing overcast, and the bright day that began at some other *now* is gone forever. Do you see? Do you see how little it matters that the gull flew away at 8:53 or that the sun went in at 9:01? *Chronos* has his uses, but he can never tell you what it is time for.

The second experience is similar. As you lose track of other people's time during a walk, other people will lose track of you. Even if they know your usual path and pace, they will be hard put to guess where you are at any given moment of their measured time. Partly because their private assessment of *chronos* will be based on the automobile, and they will have no working knowledge of the speed at which a walker proceeds. But also because they will generally be unprepared to imagine you as caught up in real *kairos*. They cannot assess the time of the watching of gulls, of the tasting of privet leaves, of the detour to catch the smell of creosote as it blows downwind from three new pilings baking in the sun. To the degree that they have a sense of their own *kairos*, they may be able to make allowances for your wanderings; but, if they are blind to everything except chronology, they will figure you wrong every time.

꒐

Place, therefore, not *space*. *Kairos*, not *chronos*. Less preoccupation with what time it is, and more questions about what it is time *for*.

But the worst error, the deadliest substitution of the abstract for the concrete, of the essential for the existential, has yet to be mentioned. It is the substitution of *legend* and *chronicle* for history. And it is deadly because it is a compound of the other substitutions and has twice the power of perversion. History (to make a start on its definition) is the shape, the meaning of events. It is the direction, the gist, of things that happen in high times at real places. It is not simply the written or verbal record of events— that is only historiography, history as known, history as a science; nor is it the foisting of interpretations on fundamentally pointless and random happenings—that describes only bad historiography, non-history, history as missed. It is not the making of a point, but the catching of a point; not the assignment of meaning, but the discovery of meaning; not the fabrication of legends about a mythical beast, but the snaring of a real one. History—existential history— *is* the beast. What men have had to say about it is only the joyful or desperate record of the chase.

It is the very wiliness of the beast—his love of peculiar dens and his fierce impatience of cages—that so often brings men home from the hunt with something other than the beast himself. It is much easier to make up legends about him than to find him; much simpler to draw abstract diagrams of where he ought to be than to grasp where he really is. And there is always a flourishing market for the legends and diagrams. The crowd around the tavern fire is quite willing to sit and listen while the theoreticians explain how all the beast's wanderings through the trackless forest are regulated by economics, or fate, or the class struggle, or the principle of evolutionary progress. And there are always plenty of woodsmen willing to give out long and detailed accounts of every inch of the forest, without

ever once showing you the beast himself. If you accept the
theoretician's word for it, you will end up with *legend*;
if you accept the woodsman's, you will have only *chronicle*.
Only a real hunter can show you history.

About the legends and the diagrams, and about what I
think is the real shape of history, I intend to say something
by and by. Whether I am a hunter or a theoretician will be
yours to decide when the time comes. Right now I want
to take the easier subject first and explain what is wrong
with *chronicle* as a substitute for history.

If I were to give you an exhaustive list of everything
I did today, together with precise spatial and chronological
coordinates for where and when I did it, you would, in one
sense, know everything about my day. But what is more
important, you would, by the same token, also know
nothing about it. That I brushed by teeth at 5:47, for
example, and saw a gull on a piling at 8:53 tells you nothing.
Either of those events could be central to my history—or
both of them irrelevant. The gull could be the lifting of a
decade of despair or just another bird; the brushing of my
teeth, an event unnoticed even by myself, or the first
morbid suggestion of cancer. History cares which; chronicle does not. History is concerned with shape, direction,
gist, singularity; chronicle jams everything into a mold.
Chronicle tries to sound like history, but it never makes it.
It is too abstract, too egalitarian, too ready to treat 5:47
as the equal of 8:53, and, therefore, too stupid to discover
meaning.

Furthermore, chronicle, as it is actually practiced, is
only the handmaid of history. Pure chronicle would be

endless and insufferable. Having no sense of judgment, no principle on which to choose among the things it is able to coordinate, it either drowns in its own data or else asks history to choose for it. The actual chronicles people compose, therefore, are really histories whose authors have ceased to think historically for themselves—who have bought a historical bill of goods without knowing it.

You have, no doubt, read history written like that, but, what is more important, you have also *heard* history—personal history—that was written like that. Take a marriage that is almost on the rocks. Whatever attempts at a common history there may have been at the start, whatever agreements there once were about the gist and direction of their relationship, they have long since failed. Husband and wife have withdrawn into separate meanings; their marriage has ceased to have a history of its own. For a while, of course, they may manage to keep a common chronicle going: they may still be able to agree that last Monday he left his socks in the sink or that yesterday she did tell him she was going shopping. But only for a while. History is the mistress of chronicle; if they live separate histories long enough, they will end up with separate and irreconcilable chronicles.

One of the things a parish priest learns early is that there are three sides to every marital disaster: his, hers, and the truth. Somewhat later in the game he comes to realize that this doesn't necessarily mean that anybody is lying, at least not consciously. He becomes accustomed to finding the couple completely unable to agree on even a single item of chronicle. The truth is not suppressed; it is undiscover-

able. The priest never does find out who puts the socks in
the sink or who picked up the carving knife first. The
events are assigned to two different people in two equally
authoritative chronicles. Nobody is lying; it is just that
history has fallen apart and chronicle has followed suit.

History, therefore, is anything but academic: the grasping of it is the central business of man's existence. First of
all, because events—the singular conjunctions of people,
places and high times—either have a shape or they do not.
If they do, it will make all the difference in the world
to man to find out what that meaning is—to get it right
instead of wrong. If they do not, then life is not only a
vapor, but a deception, and we are all kidding ourselves by
pretending to shape even a single word. The human race,
of course, does not hesitate much between the alternatives.
Most men choose to think that history exists, and all men,
except perhaps suicides, *act* as if it does. So much so, that
most of our days are spent doing something about it. We
deny it, we rewrite it, we claim the only true understanding
of it; we read it any way we like. But we read it like men
possessed.

꿩

Every person I meet has a history which threatens or
promises involvement in my history. Every thing, every
place, every time, is a mysterious conjunction, a sign to
be interpreted. This book, therefore, is about the decipher-
ing of a sacred stone—about the riddle of history. It is
about man's peculiar obsession with shape, with direction,

with meaning. About why he bothered to invent marriage
beyond sex, and friendship beyond advantage. About why
he makes towns and joins lodges; about why he paints
and whittles, about why he writes poems and fugues. About
a peculiar creature who would rather sing than shout, and
who, from the first day he learned to use words, has never
ceased to love to make them scan. Accordingly, I intend
to define man as the historical animal; as the being with a
strange thirst for the *gist* of things. I want to refresh the
sense of the priesthood of Adam, to lift up once more the
idea of man as the priest of creation, as the offerer, the
interceder, the seizer of its shape and the agent of its history.
And there is no better place to begin than where history
itself began. Listen.

*And the Lord God planted a garden eastward in Eden,
and there he put the man whom he had formed.* Why?
Why not be content to let Adam range through the open
and random places of the world? Why this garden, this
park, this *arrangement*, this shaping of creation? What
on earth was He getting at? Mightn't it be that Eden
was to be the sacrament, the sign, the effective hint of
history? Of course. The placing of man in paradise (the
word meant park, and Eden meant pleasure) was the hint
that Adam was to be nothing less than the priest of creation,
the beholder and offerer of its meaning.

*And the Lord God took the man and put him into the
garden of Eden to dress it and to keep it.* Look, Adam, he
says. Look closely. This is no jungle; this is a park. It is
not random, but shaped. I have laid it out for you this year,
but you are its Lord from now on. The leaves will fall after

the summer, and the bulbs will have to be split. You may want to put a hedge over there, and you might think about a gazebo down by the river—but do what you like; it's yours. Only look at its real shape, love it for itself, and lift it into the exchanges you and I shall have. You will make a garden the envy of the angels.

As it turned out, Adam has—and Adam hasn't. He has missed the point of creation twice for every time he has caught it once; and hovels, ruins and wars are the record of his failures. But it is the *point* that remains his preoccupation; the catching of the hint of the park is still the heart of his calling. For 75,000 years, give or take what you like, he has raked leaves and split bulbs, and he has built himself some pretty fancy gazebos. Culture—civilization—is the sum of his priestly successes, the evidence of the fulfilment of his vocation. The life of Adam is parks and plazas, and houses worthy of his priesthood; it is falling in love with the hinted garden in the world and lifting it into a paradise indeed. Though an unjust king, he is a king still; though he has failed his priesthood, he remains a priest forever. History has been his glory and history has been his shame, but the shaping of creation into the city of God remains his obsession. The Mystical Body is the point of his being.

My creek with its reeds, therefore, is not far from the truth; my walking by it is a natural exercise of my calling. I long to see it a park because Adam grew up in one. I carry my marsh reed not only with pleasure, but by right.

III The Bench Mark

Set in the sidewalk at the southeast corner of Port Jefferson harbor, halfway between the gravel yard and the icehouse, is a round bronze marker about four inches in diameter. I shall give you full particulars. In its center is a plain circle inscribed with a short line running north and south. Around this are three concentric bands of lettering. The innermost reads: $250 fine or imprisonment for disturbing this mark; the next: For elevation write to the Director, Washington, D.C.; and the last: BENCH MARK U.S. COAST & GEODETIC SURVEY.

It is some comfort to know that the powers that be are concerned to tell me where I am, but I am afraid they are too spiritual for my tastes. I am told that, if you write the Director (a grim and forbidding title: Who is he? Has he ever carried a marsh reed?), you will receive, accurate to several decimal places, the precise elevation of the plaque above mean low water. It is the old penchant for defining place in terms of space. Mean low water is like the man in the street: a handy abstraction you will never find anywhere. Look, instead, over here.

Due north from the mark is the dockside edge of the gravel yard. The harbor is calm now and the tide is out, but I have stood on this spot at other seasons. I have come

here with a crowd of my fellow townsmen—a fool among
fools, but one with them as never before—during the last
hours of a hurricane. It was a town meeting such as never
happens in the time of clocks, called to stand in the howling
wind and watch with morbid fascination while yacht after
yacht was torn from its mooring, pushed drunkenly before
the storm and pounded to pieces against the bulkheads. Later
on you could hear men entertaining each other with guesses
about how far above mean high water the harbor had
risen; but, while the storm lasted, space and *chronos* were
forgotten. This was a *place* then, a conjunction of men and
things in high time and high wind. The next morning
would be time enough for the engineers and the bankers
to assess the damage; then and there we were too much in
history to think in their terms. I am sure that no one
bothered to notice how long we watched. Small boys raced
up and down the stone heaps; men tried, foolishly and
bravely, to board a boat and start its engine; and women
with children hung back and talked about whatever it is
that women talk about at such seasons. The bench mark
has its coordinates and its uses, but the place of that conjunction was beyond its competence. Now come over here.

Walk up East Main with me. At one time it was actually
the principal street of the village, but, when the shipyards
left the center of town, another street usurped its title and
it had to be content with merely adjectival distinction.
Perhaps out of disappointment it became a backwater; for
a long time it was considered a rough neighborhood. (There
was a tavern at the lower end of it which was still open
when I first went to Port Jefferson. I can't remember its

real name, but locally it was always referred to as the
Bucket of Blood.) The roughness is pretty much gone now
and, as far as I am concerned, the street is priceless. It is the
only part of the center of the village that still qualifies as a
place. Though it has been cleaned up considerably, it still
has buildings that follow the lay of the land and speak with
voices of their own. I hope the planners take a good look
at it before they turn themselves loose.

If you start from its lower end and walk on the west
side of the street, you pass the following places: a fish
market; something that looks like a foundation (actually
it is the ruin of a truck garage cut into the side of the
hill—the roof used to be level with the sidewalk, but it was
torn off a few years back); an overgrown side yard with
a rock garden and three mysterious gravestones (after
sixteen years I still know nothing about them, and I don't
know anybody who does—a real *place* is full of mystery);
an old, narrow two-story shingle house, now empty of
people; an old, wide two-story shingle house, now full of
junk; and a space where a building used to be. Far enough.
This is what I wanted you to see.

When I first started walking, the building, though
ramshackle, was still there, and people lived in it. It was
made of brick and wood—a firetrap of unquestionable
orthodoxy. By and by, however, nobody lived in it at all,
and it began to fall apart in earnest. A couple of years
ago the property was bought by a neighbor, the building
was torn down, and the foundation filled and seeded. It
was an improvement.

But before it came down, it was gradually pierced and

disemboweled; through the broken brickwork and gaping windows you could see into the second story. There, perched in the middle of a collapsing floor, was an old iron-frame bed, painted, as it should have been, in chipped and dirty ivory. When the house went, it went too; but when I pass it now, I imagine I still see it perched there in the air, a lost piece of history—a place that was once a place, and now is nowhere. I come upon it daily as upon a scene of singular conjunctions (were they gracious or violent? were they faithful or promiscuous?); a bed of local joys and pains, a thing of high times, due seasons, last chances. Where is it now? Has it simply gone whistling down the wind into nothing?

It may be foolish of me, but I rebel at that: history so perishable, meaning so meaningless, seems hardly worth the bother. It makes our priesthood inane. The whole point of our liaisons was the weaving of a greater web; what we had in mind has always been vaster than what we had in hand. Whoever they were who entered that bed, they entered it because, somewhere in their meeting, they caught a glimpse of the web, felt a twinge of priestliness. They acted, when they most acted, because they saw themselves as ministers, as builders of a city larger and longer than themselves. It does not much matter what kind of city they willed—it may well have been a city of unreality and perversion—the point remains that, simply as human beings, as priestly agents, they could not help making history: they could not even slip between the sheets without having something in mind. Historic triumph or historic blunder, theirs was a conjunction of historic animals; if the history they made is now gone completely, it can never really have been there at all.

If all our cities go to ruin, if all our webs break and ravel, if friendship, family, law and justice survive only as long as the floorboards hold up—if the shape of the world simply flakes away like the paint on the bedstead—then man's wound is incurable. We are not sick of some alien disease that destroys our history; we are sick of history itself. It is not that the corruption of our best is our worst; it is that our very best is poison. Our deepest desire, in every one of our conjunctions, is to weave with longer threads than we can hold, to make the tapestry of history reach from east to west. But if change and decay reign supreme, the length of the threads and the vastness of the tissue are delusions. We are not weaving at all. We are only crocheting little squares for a crazy quilt that no one will last long enough to put together.

Any attempt to speak meaningfully about history, therefore, must come to grips with *change*. On the one hand, growth and transition, birth and corruption are obviously the raw material of history: in a world where nothing changed, the imposition of newer and higher shapes would not only be idle; it would be patently impossible. But, on the other hand, change is equally obviously the very thing that wrecks the shapes which man in his priestliness tries to impose: all our beds fall down. We have arrived, therefore, at a paradox. From here we go straight up or straight down; it is time to walk carefully.

As any reader of old tales knows, the only solution to a paradox is a *mystery*: the apparent either/or is the door by which the deeper magic enters the story. Unfortunately, however, the wisdom of old tales has not always been around when it was needed. True men, elves and hobbits may set their traps for mystery as soon as they smell a paradox, but a good many philosophers of history have insisted on hunting simplicities instead. Their attempts to account for the relationship between history and change have produced legends and chronicles galore, but the results have been somewhat less than satisfactory. Some of them have ended up denying change, some of them have abolished history, and almost all of them have, one way or another, taken the true agency of history away from real beings— from *things* and *persons*—and have handed it over to gods, or ghosts, or fancy mystiques.

Accordingly, the problem raised by the vanished bed on East Main Street cannot be skirted. As I promised, I shall eventually tell you more of what I think is the nature of the mystery that solves the paradox. (As a matter of fact, as evidence of good faith, I shall tip my hand right now and give it to you in code: history is saved from destruction by change because the priesthood of Adam has been enlarged through the Passion and Resurrection of Jesus into the High Priesthood of Christ. Cf., *e.g.*, Hebrews 7:24 and 25. But no more. All things in their seasons.) For the present, I want to spend a little more time on some of the solutions to the paradox which, I think, make more problems than they solve. If you do not like philosophy at all, skip to the next chapter. On the other hand, if you like your philosophy done to a fare-thee-well, you had better do the same: what follows here is too random for your taste. But, if you have the patience for it, I propose to divert you briefly, not with a complete natural history of historical errors, but with a little portfolio of philosophical field sketches. Herewith, therefore, a home-made, hand-lettered Bestiary of Unhistoric Monsters.

OCCASIONALISM

(presumed extinct, but still flourishing; specimens frequently found among the pious.)

Occasionalism is the doctrine that denies what is called secondary causation. It is a very pious sounding proposition indeed. It says that God alone is the real actor in all events —that *things* are not true causes at all, but only fronts for God. According to occasionalism, it is God who makes the eggs hatch and the leaves fall. And not simply in the sense that God made a world full of substantial beings which are then capable of acting in their own right, but in the sense that nothing except God really acts at all: only the Prime Cause *matters*. Bach did not write the D Minor Fugue; God did. Bach was only the occasion, the front. And I have not written this book, nor blown my nose, nor, to push it all the way, told my wife a lie. God did. If an occasionalist wants to make room in his system for freedom, he has to do unwarranted and illogical tricks with it. If he is consistent, he simply makes God the author of evil.

What is right about occasionalism is the clarity with which it sees the *ultimate* responsibility of God for everything. What is all wrong about it is the way it abolishes the *proximate* responsibility of individual things for everything else. It honors God by dishonoring what He made. Bach did so write the fugue—Bach himself: a real, acting, two-fisted, feet-on-the-ground *substance*; and I blew my own nose—I: a true *secondary cause*, standing gloriously *extra nihil* and *extra causas*. Occasionalism makes the world meaningless. If only God matters, if nothing on earth really changes anything, then nothing on earth makes any difference. History is a put-up job.

ESSENTIALISM

(rare and unpopular; largely driven off by existentialisms of various sorts; formerly the favorite household pet of high and dry scholasticism.)

The error of essentialism is to make too much of the abstractive power of the intellect. The mind indeed knows by grasping essences: *cat, pineapple, player piano, horse*; but essentialism, in a rapture over its ability to pickle *horse* in the juices of the mind, forgets that only existing horses are real beings. The essence *horse* has logical being: it exists in the mind; but it does not exist in reality or in any Platonic realm of pure ideas. There is, to be sure, something about actual horses that jibes nicely with it, but, for all that, *horse* is not horses. They are solid and changeable; it is immaterial and unvarying. The essentialist's world, therefore, is a world without drama and without history. It has no room for real change. It is only a stylized pageant in which changeless symbols make formal bows to each other as they pass. It is all neat and dainty; but it is a world without meetings, unfit for human habitation. It is a universe in which nothing will ever lurch toward you in love or anger, a world in which nothing *stinks*—a world in which you will never have to scrape horse manure off your shoe: the essentialist variety is odorless and remains politely in the vicinity of the horse.

Essentialism inevitably leads to a static view of reality. History is the shape of change; deny change, and you will never even begin to get near history. Yet, in the name of history, essentialism has produced some of the most changeless and non-historical monuments in the world. Disneyland. Freedomland. Places that are noplace. Places where nobody lives. Places where you can see, in all its pickled Platonic beauty, the true essence of an American town in the '90s or a frontier stockade in the Old West. Diagrams! Enclaves! Abstract forts where the siege of change can be resisted as long as the admissions roll in and the banks are happy with the mortgage. And the so-called restorations of colonial villages are no better. Restorations to what? Not to history. In the worst of them, no one is allowed to live at all. Employees in costume come in from 10:00 to 6:30 to tend the images. In the rest—in the ones that have not insulated themselves by excluding people— the real inhabitants live lives that have nothing to do with the essentialist tourist trade. Behind the abstract, early federal façade of Stony Brook lies the changing and real life

of a Levittown or a Rollingwood. Such towns may not have
a very wise view of their true history—they may have
none at all—but at least they have sense enough to keep
their distance from the essentialist pretense in their midst.

CHANCE

(common, but little understood;
the name is applied to many spec-
imens, some harmful, some not.)

Chance is the doctrine that change occurs only at random
and that meaning, therefore, is only apparent, not real. I
am not happy to have to use *chance* to describe it. I do so
only because it is the common word, and the substitutes
for it are sometimes misleading. But *chance* has such a glorious history, such a richness and viability, that I think I
shall switch to *accident* right now. In mathematics, for
example, chance has a long, meaningful and respectable
pedigree: it is not vague or accidental; it is precisely pre-
dictable. Insurance companies make money. And behind
chance, in Latin, is *fortuna*, fortune, that which occurs in
the nick of time. Next to it, in English, is luck. Noble
company! A Roman goddess and an English lady. And
nice people! Not distant proto-proto-proto-fathers like
chronos, but charming available girls who can make real
history if they set their minds to it. And, finally, there is
ordinary usage, where we speak of first chances, second
chances and last chances—all of them gorgeously, solidly
historical. I have made my mind up. I will not sully the
word. *Accident* must do its work.

The doctrine of *accidental change*, then, destroys history. And it destroys it from the ground up. So much so that nobody can write anything about a world of pure randomness, a world in which everything is an accident. The first attempts at it failed, and so have all their successors. Take Lucretius. In a treatise called *De Rerum Natura* he set out to define the world in terms of the random motion of atoms. He did very well and wrote a long book, but he gave the whole thing away at the start. In the beginning, he said, there was a perfect and parallel rain of atoms all falling in straight lines and never colliding with each other. So far so good. But where in that world does change come from? Ah, said Lucretius, what happened was that one of them swerved and bumped its neighbor, and the resulting *mêlée* set the whole world of change in motion. From there on, the system worked beautifully. With enough bumps and rattles you get elephants, mushrooms and cumquats. Behold a world built by accident! Elephants are as good as mushrooms are as good as cumquats are as good as men; lies are as good as truth, and senselessness as good as shape. It is all just bumps. There is no meaning and no history.

Ah, but did you watch his left hand closely? Did you see where that first bump came from? Of course you didn't. He couldn't show you without ruining the act. Because that bump was not random. It was unique. No matter that all the other things in his world have no explanation but accident, that one at least had a history; it caused some thing, it acted some where, it moved in *high time*. Lucretius produced a historyless system by the shabby trick of palming a real piece of history.

Eventually, as I recall, he faced up to it. He raised the question of where the first bump came from and said he just didn't know the answer. He should have stopped right then. But he didn't; and neither do the rest of his accident-mongering brethren. As I said, it would ruin the act. For the accidental view of history has to be *faked* somewhere. No one can consistently, from the ground up, present accident as the explanation of change. Somewhere they have to insert an I don't know—a disclaimer that the beginning simply was what it was: different. But if the beginning was different, why not the rest? If you have to import a historical gimmick to get started, why not try historical gimmicks all the way through? If you have to excuse the beginning by saying that's just the way things were, why not excuse the whole order by saying that's just the way things are, and get on with it—on with the serious business of facing history instead of dabbling with diagrams? *Vale, Lucreti*; you are no help at all.

FATALISM AND DETERMINISM

*(commonly supposed to be two
distinct species; on examination,
however, found to be the front
and hind ends of the same beast.)*

Fatalism and determinism both offer the same magical key to the riddle of change: everything is predetermined. Every change that has ever occurred has been the result of an already completed shape. For the fatalist, it is an unnatural, immaterial shape, a power of air and darkness against which mere things struggle in vain. For the determinist, it is a natural and material shape, working irresistibly within things from the beginning. Nothing occurs that was not built in from the start.

They are both very close to the truth, so close that it is a case of not seeing woods for trees or towns for houses. There *is* a shape. And it is not just the result of accidental collisions between things. And it *is* in some sense superior to things—outside and pulling, or inside and pushing. But there they lose it. Because the shape is not, in any simple sense, irresistible—the pulling and the pushing are more mysterious than that. And it is not just inside or just outside —it is strangely both. The occasionalist was wrong when he made God the only actor; how much more these two, when they make fate or mechanism the only actor. They have misread the play. Fate and mechanism are not actors at all. Fate will be lucky if he can get a job as prompter; and mechanism should be happy he is a stagehand. God, of course, is an actor, but not the way the occasionalist thinks. Apart from His role as author and producer—in which He takes exceptional care to stay out of the play and let His creatures stand proudly on whatever feet He gave them— He shows up as a protagonist only mysteriously, as a *thing* among other things: in the children of Israel, for example, or, supremely, in the *humanity* of Christ. He appears to insist that the drama of history be played out by creatures themselves—by men and women, wood and steel, mountains, rivers, rain and sand. He will not allow them to be fronts for anybody.

The error of fatalism and determinism, therefore, is to do just what God refuses to do: to take the responsibility for history away from things and to park it somewhere else. They invent outside forces or built-in mystiques and make them the real actors in the play. They claim to have discovered a formula which, if it could have been known, would infallibly have predicted all things. They can write you the recipe for history without having to look at history at all.

That, of course, is just thinly veiled occasionalism. They may posit mystiques where occasionalism posits God, but the end result is the same. In place of sly little trap doors between the inside of God's mind and the inside of things, they run hidden wires to every existing being—economic wires, physical wires, fatalistic wires, psychological wires— and then insist that it is the current in the wires, and not the things themselves, that make history. But that is to make an even worse shipwreck than before. Bad enough that occasionalism should make things a front for God; worse ten times over that we should turn them into patsies for a lot of abstract and mindless forces.

Out with all the occasionalisms, then, whether divine, fatalistic or deterministic. It is *things* that make history, not forces, not mystiques—not even God in any simple sense. Just real beings acting for themselves within the real but mysterious purpose of a graceful and competent creator; things solid enough to act out of their own natures, and a God sure enough of His power to give them their head. Mysterious? Of course. If they had been willing to admit mystery, they would not have run afoul of mystique.

PANTHEISM

*(a monster; rare in its pure state,
but widespread in hybrid forms;
sometimes attractive, always dangerous.)*

One word only. Pantheism is occasionalism without God.
If occasionalism *with* God makes nonsense of history, how
much more pantheism, whose god is only the sum total of
all the occasions—a kind of cosmic chronicle which omits
nothing, prefers nothing, loves nothing, and hates nothing.
It is a diagram of indifference, a dark and illegible legend.
Out with it! Ugh!

EVOLUTIONARY SUPERSESSION

*(the most commonly domesticated
of all the beasts; the sacred cow
of modern man.)*

Evolutionary Supersession is my own fancy name for the
extension of the biological hypothesis of evolution to every
other subject under the sun: history, art, science, language,
architecture. In stigmatizing it, I have no intention of attacking the biological hypothesis itself. The history—and
the idiocies—of the nineteenth-century clerical sport of
Darwin-baiting are still too fresh in people's minds to give
me any hope of being understood if I did. About evolution
itself, therefore, I offer no criticisms, only a caution: evolu-

tion is not the same thing as destiny; it is, at best, only a description of one of the ways in which *things* make history. The mystery of the shaping of the world cannot safely be reduced to *any* mystique—especially not to a transformist one. Evolution may indeed be crucial to the mystery—may be the left and right legs on which it runs and leaps; but in a sane definition it will be seen only as the body of the mystery, not as its soul and substance.

The caution is, I think, necessary. The modern world is so used to equating evolution with history that it quickly misreads even the most expert handling of the subject. It assumes almost automatically that the final destiny of the world is a matter of the mere working out of built-in transformist processes. Take, for example, Teilhard de Chardin's concept of the Omega Point. It is frequently assumed to be a kind of glorious last stop on the railroad of creation—someplace that the world will arrive at quite on its own steam. Yet, as far as I can see, the Omega Point is simply Teilhard's evolutionary way of talking about what I have referred to as the fulness of the mystery of the City. As a matter of fact, on a fair view of all his writing, it turns out to be none other than Christ the Incarnate Word mightily and sweetly ordering all things: Teilhard is as far from mere mystique as the Bible is. But such is the fascination of the transformist epic that his commentators, as often as not, set him forth as the supreme vindicator of evolution as the key to history.

My point is that he isn't; and that evolution simply can't do the work they set for it. What it really accomplishes is a good deal of mischief. The habit of equating history with evolution makes disastrous alterations in the way man looks at the world. Just allow evolution as a mystique to become the interpretive principle in any field and, in proportion to the extent of its application, the true shape and history of the subject will vanish from sight.

For what does it do? It offers itself as a master key for discovering the shape of change. Once a man adopts it, he promptly acquires a penchant for thinking not about the real history of things, but about the evolutionary shape they are supposed to have. He begins by seeing what comes earlier as a provisional, a transitional, version of what comes later. Then he finds himself looking on the earlier as explainable only in the light of the later. And finally he discovers he is unable to assign any intrinsic and abiding importance to the earlier, since its truest function was to be superseded by the later. One disclaimer. I am by no means ruling out the fact of change, or the possibility of a legitimate doctrine of development. I am only saying that evolutionary supersession makes things in themselves meaningless, and that it makes real history indecipherable. It is a key all right, but it does not fit the lock of the actual world.

More than that, it contains the seed of its own destruction. By its constant insistence that the meaning of the earlier is discoverable only in the later, it effectively cuts itself off from discovering any meaning at all. It is very well to say that the earlier phases of a science or an art are important chiefly because they can be seen in the light of today's syntheses, but only the shortest-sighted among us can fail to see that the evolutionary saw that thus fells Thomas Aquinas, Telemann, Newton and the harpsichord, cuts off the branch we are sitting on as well. If the past is important only as transitional to the present, then the present is important only as transitional to the future: the much touted evolutionary meaning of history turns out to be one that never arrives. As a matter of fact, the evolutionary view of history never does come up with *meaning*. It starts with a *mystique* of improvement and, thousands of years later, it makes an end, with the mystique still beautifully intact, but with no way of allowing anything but the contemporary to matter. Mercifully, few people apply it consistently: while they are tearing down old buildings with one hand, they are holding an old novel with the other. But, insofar as it is applied at all, it plays hob with history. For it is not an approach to history. It is a mystique of the modern, a cult of the contemporaneous. For all its devices, it never escapes from the purblindness that leads men to think today's hemlines the only right ones.

A quick and exceedingly partial list of instances in which it has done its damnedest.

The facile economic evolutionism that sees property only as an institution to be superseded. The glib assertion, mostly by non-scientists, that Newtonian physics is dead. The prejudice, among cellists and flutists, against gambists and recorderists. Silly things said about the lute by people who have never heard Dowland played by Julian Bream; idiocies uttered about Giotto being transitional to Masaccio, and Masaccio an unevolved Michelangelo, by people who apparently can't see that Giotto thought he was a painter in his own right.

The past stood for itself; if you take it as transitional, you preclude the discovery of its meaning. Its history escapes as you write it. If they would only content themselves with working up a good doctrine of development, they might have a chance of discovering something about politics or painting or music or the history of science. But they insist on evolution, and, as a result, they massacre the past. Their watchword is: No prisoners!

One other instance. The history of language, seriously and factually contemplated, defies evolutionary explanation. To be sure, the drug-store encyclopedias and the little (and not so little) school science texts still hand out the grunt-and-groan theory of the origin of language. They leap from the *oogle umph* of the savage to the prose of John Donne with scarcely a strain. Evolution accounts for it all. What they never seem to see is that no known savage has ever been caught with a vocabulary limited to *oogle umph*; that it is precisely in the early stages of a language that you are likely to find more complicated accidence, and that most historical languages, if they can be ascertained to run in any direction at all, seem actually to run downhill.

Language, almost more clearly than anything else in the world, refuses to have even its poorest specimens written off as of transitional importance only. Every known instance of it, from the best to the worst, looks more like a game played for its own sake, like something that would matter even if never another word were said. The real growth of English, for example, is not evolutionary, but developmental; not the endless succession of transitional forms, but the slow and continuous building of a city of speech, the age-long addition of monument after monument to the real and enduring fabric of the metropolis of the English tongue.

What is needed is a moratorium on evolutionary explanations and an honest attempt at another, and more merciful, doctrine of development. The evolutionary interpretation of history is gratituous: *post hoc* is not necessarily *propter hoc*; it could just as well be *propter* something else of vastly greater mysteriousness. The successions of history make more sense when understood in a way which does not destroy the past. The early and the late are better seen as the spreading suburbs of an old and growing city than as discrete and transitional individuals which ceaselessly replace each other. For what it is worth, therefore, I give you the doctrine of the Mystery of the City as my contribution to a sane concept of development.

Take the whole tissue of any science. Take theology, for example. We have our share of the evolution-mongers. They keep howling for a modern theology to suit the modern world. They are quite prepared to discard the theological past as so much useless baggage. But they are wrong. The former and latter theologians of the church are, all of them, more intelligible if they are taken not as each other's precursors and successors, but as earlier and later builders, each of whom did his work, left his monument and went to his reward. True enough, some of those monuments—Arius', for example, or Novatian's—have been submitted to the wrecker's ball, and better structures built in their places. But others have been left to stand as seemly and useful buildings. On the evolutionary theory this is unintelligible

—only the latest suburb is fit for modern habitation. But on a sound doctrine of development the whole city of theology remains our rightful territory. The real history of theology, therefore, is not an endless supersession of opinions, but the slow disclosing of the true shape of a city.

Or take the history of the natural sciences. The hint of the fundamental formula for relativity turns out to have been buried all along in one of the oldest buildings in mathematics: the Pythagorean Theorem. Einstein does not supersede Pythagoras; he is his fellow citizen—and in no mean city. At the age of ten, Einstein rejoiced when he heard the theorem and proved it on his own; as for Pythagoras himself, he sacrificed one hundred oxen the day he discovered it. That is history. It carves change into useful shapes. Evolutionary supersession is a dull tool. It simply butchers meaning.

Or, finally, take Port Jefferson. It sits by its harbor like the woman at the well—it has had many shapes, and the shape it now has is not its own. Bounded by hills, set down on its salt marsh, it has failed to be a city more often than it has succeeded. But its failures have been always—have been precisely—failures to become *itself*, to find Port Jefferson in Port Jefferson. Its history has consisted largely of the missing of its history; but it has never stopped trying. And it cannot: it has eyes. If it will only keep them open, they will tell it all it needs to know. They will tell it, of course, that it has not found it—anyone with eyes can see that; but they will also tell it that its history is still waiting to be found, and anyone with eyes can see that too. Home is where we start from. If the day ever comes when we get it right, we will rejoice in the discovery of something that was there all along. With Pythagoras we shall sacrifice one hundred oxen.

Do you see what that means? It means that history is not simply the building of the city or the finding of the city; it is *the growth of the city in a high mystery*. It means that there are no short cuts. No neat little mystiques that will make it pop up automatically; no fancy fates that will drop it down, ready-to-install, from the realm of pure ideas; not even a God who will push it down your throat willy-nilly. It will indeed grow up from the earth, but not by a mystique; and it will indeed in some sense come down from heaven, but not by miracle. It will grow up in the mystery of the real and substantial interactions of things that can act for themselves; and it will come down in the mystery of an omnipotence that rules by grace and not by force. When it comes for the first time, it will have been here long since; when it comes for the last, it will be, astonishingly, the same thing.

Have I given my whole case away? Have I locked the mystiques out of the front door only to let them in at the back? I don't think so. It is *mystery* that saves me. But mystery in earnest, not just puzzle. Mystery as God's inscrutable way of doing business. Mystery as the way he steers the bicycle of history with his hands in his pockets. Nobody is shoved, nothing is jimmied; nothing need ever be anything but true to itself. *He never even touches the handlebars!* Pilate is Pilate and Caiaphas is Caiaphas; Peter is Peter, and John is John; the soldiers are soldiers, and the women are themselves; the nails are iron, and the cross is wood. All in their own natures, all acting for themselves: the creatures of a God powerful enough not to have to use inside mystiques or outside clubs; of a God who can afford *anything*; of a God who can do nothing but hang there and still ride history home no-hands.

IV The Renegade Priest

VERY well, then: mystery as the key to change. And mystery *neat*—not mystery and water. Not the diluted kind that solves the case by saying it was only the butler that did it, but the full-strength solution whose last unnerving word is that the butler was really an archangel in disguise.

But is that a fair answer? Does it give even the sympathetic listener any smallest crust to gnaw on? Do you not have a right to wonder whether it is being used to excuse mere mystification? Granted that the heart of mystery must by nature remain within the veil, may you not still reasonably ask to finger the cloth a little? If you are told you cannot hope to see the mystery face to face, is there not at least some cleft in the rock where you can hide as it passes and catch a glimpse of its back parts—of the angle of its hat or the style of its walking?

There is. And you have seen it already: the space left by the demolished building on East Main Street.

The bed in the air, you recall, was a piece of history which had been lost from sight; and it was, by that very fact, a challenge to the possibility of any history whatsoever. If things that once were thought to matter supremely can, by the simple process of physical change, cease to matter at all, then something is wrong somewhere. Either we were mistaken about the mattering or we were mistaken about its disappearance; but one half of the dilemma has got to give. My own bias, of course, is clear, and I propose to follow it: we were right the first time. Things do matter, they do *mean*; the inveterate human assumption that man has something to *do* with history is no delusion. When we write, when we sing, when we tell children not to leave juice glasses on the piano; when we flirt, when we cry, when we marry, when we burn—we are not just kidding ourselves. We were meant to mean: shape and history are our native air.

But how do you prove it? What do you look at to see it? The question comes back stronger than ever: If that history is saved, where is it? And this time the answer, though still a mystery, begins at least to show the sleeves of its shirt. In the emptiness between two buildings we brush against a singular bit of weaving, a piece of cloth with a strange and exciting *hand*: the bed in the air was one of the conjunctions of the city. It may now be gone, but its connections run forward and backward into the web of history. And not only that. The couple who lay in it were priestly beings: if they still exist, the offering they made of each other still stands, for good or ill. Two facts, therefore: the fact of the material existence of the web and the fact of the continued being of the priestly creatures who wove it. A left sleeve and a right. Not the mystery itself, of course, but at least some solid vestiges of its clothing. *Presences*, not just hopes. Two contacts with something that demands more than a shrug in reply—something to which the only possible answer is: *Who's there?*

Consider first the left sleeve: the *web* left by the mystery of change. Individuals replace each other constantly, but the city remains with us. The bed in the air has long since vanished, but the history of that bed persists: it is extended beyond itself in the fabric of the city—it has continued to *mean*, to make a difference. And it has continued in a way that is very plain and old fashioned: it has had physical and moral consequences; biologically and personally it remains the source of blessings and curses. Perhaps, for example, the marrige in that bed was fruitful. Children went from it into histories of their own. But they went endowed by *its* history. Bright or dull, kind or cruel, rich or poor, sick or whole, they proceeded forth as all things must: from other things—the heirs or victims of their origin. The bed from which they sprang was a conjunction of the web of history; the threads that met there crossed, joined and continued on into the tissue of their lives. Their I.Q.'s, their blood types, their pigmentation, their accent came to them trailing long warps from a past that does not even need to be known to be received.

What is all this but the city? To say it is a very primitive aspect of the city is to leave it a city nonetheless. But to say that it is nothing but itself is to miss the point altogether. The very fact of physical change is the first hint of something beyond physical change: continuity. Nothing moves itself. The threads are precisely the threads of a web; relationship is an intimation of the city. And it defies reduction to meaninglessness. Even the biological and geological stones of the city will not keep their peace at that. The fact of physical causation will not let itself be taken for granted.

The whole will not be reduced to its parts. To say that I.Q. is only genes, or eye color only Mendel's law, is impossible. Why *only*? Cloth is not only threads; it is weaving. The real problem is why are there genes at all, why Mendel's law? The ultimate question is: *Who's there?* To let it go at genes is like being kissed in the dark and saying it was only a kiss in the dark. Any man who can do it should be suspect. He has found a lipstick-stained cigarette on an uninhabited island and has gone back to counting clam shells.

Or take it up a notch. The people who lay in that bed either grew in love or shrank in hate, and their love or their hate went forth with power. They grew up in the shadow of the beds that preceded them, and their own bed cast its shadow on their children's history. Again, long warps. Shuttles that cross and recross the loom. Blessings. Curses. Real gifts—gracious or sinister. How many generations of mishandling did it take to leave him unable to love a woman, or her unwilling to hold her tongue? Or how far down the web will the thread of her pity run, and where will his patience not extend its rule?

The first hint of the city, therefore, lies in the real transmissions that occur between things—in the *exchanges* that make up the tissue of history. We stand in a world of discrete individuals, but in all that world no individual is separate from the rest. Genetically, morally, legally, economically, we are members one of another. Even the left sleeve of the mystery is a marvel of weaving, a tissue of coinherence.

And if the physical web of being is such, how much

more the other sleeve, the web formed by man's priestly oblation of the world? For beyond the concrete transmissions—well past the comparative simplicity of the blessings and curses—lie the vast complexities of the city as it is lifted up by the priesthood of Adam and held within the tissue of the mind. Having picked my bone with essentialism, I have no further argument with knowledge. In its true place it can hardly be exalted too much. It is the glory of man, the chief vessel of his priesthood. Our disasters are due to its perversion, not its use.

I have a black-and-tan hound who walks with me every day. He answers, when he likes, to the name of Tom. It is now illegal, even in Port Jefferson, to walk a dog without a leash, but I do it anyway. As a matter of fact, I consider walking a dog an outrage—on man and beast. Dogs are creatures in their own right; they must act for themselves, not be operated by men. They must walk, not *be walked*. Tom and I proceed through our village in an equality. It is his as much as it is mine. And it is his in a way that cannot be mine except through my priesthood as man. Sometimes, when we come to the foot of town, he leaves me and I do not see him again for hours. My path and his diverge; we follow separate threads through the tissue of the city. My way lies along streets, but his along tracks that even boys cannot follow. Across yards, past hedges, over the sandlots and through the creek he traces the pattern of his going; and in the wonder of his animal knowledge, he sees and remembers, and learns the way. (There are days on which, my children tell me, he hangs around the school—a good mile from the house—just before the buses leave. Even when my wife has driven the children home herself, he invariably arrives before them.)

My reaction to all this is wonder and delight. There is a Port Jefferson about which I know nothing except through Tom. It is a city of another size and shape, a set of unimaginable vistas and detours. And my wonder and delight are only heightened by the fact that Tom himself knows so little about what he knows. He can beat an automobile home—he is master of this city as few men are—and yet he does not know it as a *city*. He can navigate the web, but he will never *think* of it. That is my office—mine as Adam the priest of creation. The meeting of his threads and mine are mine alone to see. If the city grows because of Tom, it will be because Tom's knowledge has been taken up in mine.

And from there it is only a step to other threads, and to conjunctions like the sand of the sea.

At one of the gravel docks, huge stones are currently being lifted from barges and loaded on flat-bed trucks. No one here now seems to know much about them. They are a subject for speculation. Where do they come from? Where are they going? A city of men, in its natural and casual approach to mysteries, chats idly about them. But it chats by necessity; for the paths of those stones are more lines in the web, more tracings of city upon city. The inquiry is a priestly quest, the search for a handhold on the shuttle by which they are woven into the fabric of history.

As a matter of fact, my own knowledge of them is slightly more extensive. They were quarried, I presume, somewhere up the Hudson, hewn from their ancient places in a city of hills and floated downriver through the Sound to this harbor. The trucks, I understand, take them to Montauk, or Westhampton, or someplace out east to be set down on the edge of the land in an attempt to achieve the shaping of still another city. There they will lie in great stone groins built out into the sea. From the ribbing of their first city into the groins of a second, and only I—Adam—know it. The web is built ceaselessly, but it is man alone that sees it and lifts it up. The city comes to fruition only by his priesthood.

It is vast beyond dreams. Even in the fibres of one man's being, it extends to the corners of creation. What do I hold within me for lifting, for oblation? The passing smell of coffee roasters on a dark day in lower Manhattan. Sunlight on Lake Michigan, and the waves lapping at still other groins. Rain on the tenement-lined streets off First Avenue, where Stuyvesant Town has since reared its head. The forever vanished slashes of sunlight shining down through the tracks of the old Third Avenue El.

Man was meant to love the city and to lift its exchanges beyond themselves; to grasp its weaving and to feel its *hand*. Not simply to be the lover of beauty, but the lover of being, just because it *is*. For it is *ens inquantum ens* that is the root of beauty, goodness and truth, and of the oneness that is the raw silk of the tissue of the city. But it is Adam the priest who alone can see its threads for what they are and weave them, through their crossings and conjunctions, into history.

ಳಿ

Two hints so far, therefore, of the outline of the mystery: its operation in things by the mute but eloquent fact of change, and its operation in man by the lifting of the web into his knowledge as history. It is a beginning. But it is no place to stop. It raises as many questions as it solves. Granted that the mystery seems present in things and in man, how do you know it is not just an appearance? First of all, what of the misshapings of history, what of man's endless years of wrong history and bad history? If man loves shape so well, why does he wreck it so often? Should we not expect so great a mystery to be somewhat more successful? And, secondly, what about the fact that the priest of the mystery—man—can hold the city together only as long as he can hold himself together? Man's knowledge is as wide as all history, but it goes out when his brain goes out. He dies. The marvelous device which held the city in the conjunctions of its wires goes into the ground —is disconnected, disassembled and junked. Where is meaning *then*? Have we only discovered the marks of the mystery to lose them again in a darker forest? Have we built a dike against unmeaning only to have it destroyed by the pressure of the waters it contains?

It is important not to give too fast a reply. There are so many cheap answers in circulation, and so many trite and inadequate versions of the expensive one, that it is more helpful to try to state the problems in detail before delivering any—even the best—precut solution. The problems, of

course, are the old riddles of Sin and Death: the twin results of Adam's fall, and the immemorial destroyers of the
history he always seeks and so seldom gets right. Consider
death first.

Even if the web of being actually exists in the mute
changing of the physical world, it does not really *matter*—
enter history—until it is grasped by the priesthood of man
and lifted up beyond itself. If there is not a mind around
capable of taking in its meaning, there is very little sense
in talking about meaning at all. But if each of the minds
that grasps history is capable only of a temporary grip,
if shape and meaning can be blown out, as they are, in
death after death around the clock and world without end,
what good is the grasp of history in the first place?

Ah, you say, but things are not that bad. Individual
minds may die, but the succession of minds goes on. The
tissue of history lives by its wits. With a little agility, it
will manage, by written word or spoken, to find itself
new minds, new houses, before the old ones cave in. But
be careful. You are on the verge of a cheap answer.

In the first place, it is hardly even a half-truth. Only the
smallest part of any man's grasp of history can be transmitted. He may, by dint of a lifetime of talk, communicate
some of what he has grasped to other minds; he may even,
in the farthest reaches of poetry, succeed in transmitting
much of it. But *all*? Never. The determinative flashes of
sunlight on cobblestones, the instants of anger and minutes
of tenderness that are integral to the shape he knows the
world to have—the thousand impressions that have flowered
into meaning for him—remain radically incommunicable.

On the day he dies, a hundred chapters will go into the rubbish for every one he leaves in someone else's desk. History—grasped history—can indeed be transmitted; but not enough of it to take the edge off the horror of unmeaning. My history's survival in other men's minds is carrion comfort. It is peace with oppression; consenting to the destruction of a city at the price of the preservation of a bungalow. The consolation is too small for such a loss.

Nevertheless, when a John Kennedy dies—when any famous man falls under the sentence—the leader writers trot it out as the principal string of their bow. He may be gone from us, they mourn, but his words and works will live as long as man himself draws breath. They mean well; but it simply will not do. Of all that was disconnected by the assassin's bullet, far too little remains. John Kennedy was a priest offering the world in the sanctuary of his mind. And so are Nathan Cohen and you and I. The enormity of the destruction of such temples is hardly lessened by the knowledge that four stones and two third-class relics of a priest are on view in some foreign country. It helps a little, but not much.

Furthermore, the survival of history in the minds of successive generations is unacceptable from the point of view of the priest himself. It is not only that so much of the history I have lifted up will go into the discard with my body; far worse is the fact that it is *my* oblation which will be lost. What I have seen and loved has been lifted up for *it*self and for *my*self, not for entombment in an abstract racial consciousness. I have run my own fingers over the fabric of the world; my offering has been precisely mine: the oblation of my own heart's astonishment. If that goes for good, I can hardly be blamed for looking down my nose on the consolation that someone else will offer in my stead. Death is the unfrocking of Adam the priest. That is why we cry at funerals: because poor old John will never in this world be allowed to say Mass again; never again lift up the beings around his table, never be permitted to run his own hands across the silk of his friendships or the burlap of his pains. Small comfort that there are still other priests to offer; *his* offering is gone, and the loss is inconsolable.

The cheap answer, therefore, will not do. If there is any hope for history, it will not lie in books or other minds. If there is ever to be an answer to the problem of Death, it will have to deal with death itself. Meaning can be saved only by the lifting of the sentence under which Adam stands.

And the same is true of the problem of Sin. Either the misshaping of history will be seen as a remediable perversion of man's natural love of shape, or it will destroy shape altogether. But again, before any attempt at presenting the answer to sin, must come an effort to understand how sin entered in the first place.

When you have lost an idea, a hint of meaning, you can sometimes find it by retracing your steps. You get up in the morning, perhaps, you brush your teeth, you shave, you dress; and, as you do, you arrive at the formulation of a brilliant gambit for attacking a problem. Downstairs then, and to breakfast. But over your second cup of coffee, you discover that the flash of insight has escaped you: *that* you thought of it, you are sure; *what* it was you thought of, you cannot remember at all. The only thing for it is to go back, to walk once again through the rooms in which it first occurred. And you do. And somewhere between the toothpaste and the shaving cream, between the trousers and the socks, the meaning returns as good as new.

So also here. If the first hint of history was given by the placing of man in a *park*, a paradise, an Eden, that is the place to walk through again to find it.

The park, then, was Adam's to behold, to lift and to offer. It was in the garden that he first saw shape; and it is in the garden also that the first hint of the misshaping rears its head. *But the serpent was more subtil than any beast of the field.* Ah! And he said, *Yea, hath God said, Ye shall not eat of every tree of the garden?* Ah! Yes. That was it.

God says to Adam: See what I have made you. Behold a creation with a shape that cries for shaping, with a meaning waiting to be meant by somebody. I challenge you to a game of oblation. My serve first. Watch now! Watch trees and grass, watch earth and mountains and hills; watch wells, seas and floods, and whales and all that move in the water. Catch! Catch beasts and cattle and children of men; catch winter and summer and frost and cold; catch nights and days and lightnings and clouds; catch *omnia opera Domini*—catch them, and return the service!

And Adam says to God: Wait a minute; I didn't hear you mention that tree over there. And God's jaw drops.

Look, Adam, he says, that's only the foul line. Forget it; it's just a rule. I have my reasons for it, but it's in a good place, believe me. If I can provide the court and the game, trust me to make the rules to play it by. After all, you haven't even returned the service yet. Try it again—my serve.

And once more, across the net of the world, come ice and snow and light and darkness, fire and heat and dews and frosts, winds of God and fowls of the air, and *omnia germinantia in terra.* And this time Adam throws down his racquet, and with an edge to his voice says: But what about that tree?

Do you see? The wrath of God is only his exasperation at a player who will not watch, at a partner who will not return the service. It is the divine *good grief!* over the purblindness of a creature who would rather argue about the foul line than play the game. There is your answer to why the game of history has gone so badly: Adam is *in* the game, but not *with* it. He could play if he wanted, but he would rather score debating points of his own. He is a priest who will not return the service.

Mercifully, though, it has not turned out quite as badly as it might. Sin is strong enough to spoil history, but not strong enough to wreck it altogether. There is just too much shape in the world, and too much love of shape in man, for history to fail completely. Even a carping Adam has had his moments. The glory that was Greece and the grandeur that was Rome, and the joys of open-eyed court-ship and the delights of the city of the sciences have not altogether gone begging. Culture is the record of what priestly success he has had. That it is a tarnished record is sad; but that it exists at all is the proof of his priesthood.

And more. Even his failures are priestly. The slavery upon which the ancient world was built was a wrong oblation within the city. The building of the Third Reich upon the extermination of the Jews was a wicked offering, the perversion of a priesthood that should have held them for themselves and lifted them into the city. Such things prove history in the very act of destroying it. The sins by which man has ruined the shape of the world are precisely the acts of a spoiled priest: resentment, prejudice, envy, hate; lust, greed, sloth, pride. Sin is not accidental or irrelevant: it is the oblation of the right things in the wrong way. It is the very best in man that wrecks the world. The riddle of a misshapen creation must be solved not by despairing of that best, but by the healing of it in the renewal of the priesthood of Adam.

❦

There is, admittedly, one part of the mystery that will remain a mystery forever: Why did God make man a priest in the first place? The only honest answer is as mysterious as the mystery itself: he was pleased to have us so. Beyond that no man can go. But even that is a hint at which the heart leaps up. *He was pleased!* We are what we are not out of necessity, but out of delight. For all the disasters of its history, the world is still a *lark*, a game into which we are invited by God. That the game has gone badly counts as nothing as long as the invitation still stands. And if, beyond the mere invitation, he has actually promised some day to restore us to our true priesthood . . . well, that is a hope worth any waiting: a day not only for you and me, but for Tom and the marsh reeds and for all the beds of our conjunctions; a day for the triumphant proclamation of the web, and for the building of Jerusalem in a green and pleasant land.

V Interlude in the Garden

You are free to receive with joy or reject with horror what comes next. I accept, sight unseen and with equanimity, whatever theological or philosophical stickers you see fit to fasten on me. Whether I am a fundamentalist, or a liberal—or both, or neither—is mine to know and yours to find out, and, having found out, to ease me in or out of your scheme of things accordingly. I am in your hands.

Since the garden, Adam has worked at his priesthood by whatever fits and starts he could manage. There is very little in creation he hasn't taken a notion to do something about. He has done things up, done things over, and done things in; but, well or badly, he has done. And his doing has been a *historical* pursuit. The definition of man as the historical animal is not only as good as any; it is better than most. He is the priest of the world, the being whose life is a search for shape, an obsession to draw what he loves *into* his history and to cast what he loathes *out of* it. I propose, therefore, to take a closer look at the details of his oblation. But since the scope of his priesthood is so vast—since we are so regularly more staggered than settled by it—I shall do the job by halves. In subsequent chapters I shall dwell first on his lifting of *things* into history; then, a little later, I shall come to the way in which he lifts up more complicated beings: *persons*.

But first I want to make a detour—to draw a longish line under something I think makes a difference. I have talked about the creation of Adam as the introduction of a priestly—a historical—being into the world; and I have talked about the fall of Adam as his failure to exercise his priesthood—as a disaster in the history department of creation. What needs to be added now is an insistence that the priesthood of Adam cannot be just a historical principle: Adam himself, in his creation and in his fall, has to have been a historical fact. No matter how many fine and fancy meanings we may be able to draw out of his historicality, it must also have a plain meaning: somewhere along the line, somebody showed up at a real time and place as the first of a race of priestly beings.

I feel I am about to lose my audience. I shall give you one disclaimer. I am not at all concerned here with whether that somebody was a *he* or a *they*, or whether he was made in one shot, or gradually pasted up over millions of years. The only point I want to make is that if you seriously intend to see history as a real web, then the web itself must have a beginning, *and that beginning must be discussed historically*. No one should be dispensed from the attempt to write Genesis; and no one ever is. Admittedly, neither scientists nor theologians have reporters' notes on the event, so everybody has to do the job imaginatively; but it is precisely that job that everyone has to do, scientists as well as theologians. There is no real choice about Adam. The only open question is whether we will do him, and the rest of history which follows from him, justice.

I bring this up because a great deal of solemn nonsense

has been bandied about on the subject. In the interest of making a hasty accommodation between a stale biblical chronology and a half-baked theory of universal evolution, all kinds of things were said by all kinds of people. On the one hand, biblical obscurantists made a frantic attempt to salvage the chronology by sweeping scientific knowledge under the rug. On the other, modernist theologians retreated so hurriedly before the specter of evolutionary supersession that they abandoned wholesale the theology and horse sense of the Scriptures. The first have, mercifully, met the fate they deserved; but the second are still with us. They have such a fear of sounding like Genesis that they end up sounding like gibberish. They are so afraid of making Adam a particular man that they forget that, if history is real, some particular man will have to turn out to have been Adam. In the day of judgment we may find out that his wife called him Oscar and that he lived in a Norwegian fiord; but it will be only a detail. He himself will have existed. And the essential historical fact about him will be not simply that our biological inheritance came from him, but that *all* the threads of the web began with him. It is precisely the rest of history that you lose if you unload Adam.

You think I am tilting with windmills. But consider. Do you really think that the objection to the Adam of Genesis was based on a scholarly unwillingness to accept Bishop Ussher's word that man first appeared on a Friday morning in 4004 B.C.? I do not. That was only the particular sandbar on which they finally ran aground. If it had not been that, it would have been something else. Their

real trouble lay in the fact that they (and we) had been
sailing for several centuries in the shoal waters of a non-
historical view of history.

Under the influence of what they conceived to be the
demands of evolution, they took to expounding both the
creation story and the narrative of the fall as myths. And
by *myth* they meant something quite specific: a fundamentally non-historical truth, presented under the guise
of fictitious history. (There is, admittedly, a historical
way of using myth—it can also mean an imaginative, but
not unlikely, reconstruction of an event which really happened but went unrecorded at the time—but that is not
what they had in mind.) The story in Genesis became, in
their hands, only a diagram of the spiritual state of Every-
man; they lived in mortal terror of ever allowing Adam
to be anyone's grandfather.

And, yet, that is the crucial point. Adam has *got* to be
someone's grandfather, or history is nonsense. The race of
man is precisely a web: times without number, good science
has done nothing but confirm that. If I got my flat-footed
walk or my love of lead foil from my own grandfather,
the case is closed. History is by that fact real; and all real
things have beginnings. My grandfather himself had a
grandfather. And if you rummage around long enough,
somewhere in the web you are going to run into a fellow
who had no human grandfather and who, therefore, is the
real grandaddy of history. That gentleman is Adam.

Why, then, were the theologians so afraid of talking
theologically about the beginning of the web? Why were
they so scared of Adam? For two reasons. First, because

they had an exaggerated view of the apologetic value of intellectual fashionableness; but secondly, and chiefly, because they had long since ceased seriously to think about the tissue of history. Evolution, as a built-in mystique, had conned them out of it. They were so awed by the supposed extent to which man had changed that they felt guilty about saying anything definite about his origin. And so they invented one of the most insidious distinctions in the history of anthropology: the division of man into historic and pre-historic. Admittedly, it has a legitimate meaning: man after historiography as opposed to man before historiography. But in the popular mind the effect of it was to divorce *us* (men) from *them* (missing links) and, by leaving us without any theological estimation of our actual beginning, to rob us of a true view of the rest of the web of history.

The fuss about the historicity of Adam, therefore, is essential. The human race has lived under the compulsion of history for as long as it can remember: it has been obsessed with shape and meaning from the start. No theory of the origin of man is worth a plugged nickel unless it can make room for meaning *at the start.*

Adam is inseparable from the web. He is the priest of creation, the agent of the mystery of the city. There is not a man in the world who doesn't grapple with meaning all his life. To omit the discussion of meaning from the account of his origin, therefore—to allow it to wander in the middle of the piece like an orphan of the storm—is to leave it an orphan forever. If meaning arrived late, it never arrived at all; you cannot derive something from nothing. It would have been better not to talk about the subject at all than to dodge the issue by beating up on Genesis. Whoever wrote it was a theologian and historian of the first magnitude. If you don't like the way he did it, you are welcome to try making up your own version. But don't think you can just sit on the sidelines and throw stones. You can't write history without talking about beginnings.

But the insistence upon the historicity of Adam is not justified simply by the necessity of a historical account of the creation of man. It becomes supremely important in the narrative of the Fall. The Scriptures, you recall, make no bones about the historicity of *that* either. God made man and set him in the garden; and man, for a short while at least, lived in a state of goodness before he went sour. Modern theologians, however, almost to a man, throw up their hands at that. The evolutionary notion that man has slowly risen out of meaningless savagery into meaningful history has so captured their minds that they find the notion of a historical time of innocence simply unthinkable. If they comment at all on the story of the temptation, they do it by trotting out their Adam-is-Everyman fowling piece and blasting the history out of it. But two can play that game. I have here an Adam-has-got-to-be-Somebody squirrel rifle, and I intend to use it. History must not go undefended. Stand back.

There is only one person you can blame (or thank) for putting meaning into the world: God is the only possible author of history; man didn't make himself any kind of animal, let alone a priestly one. But there are two people you might blame for taking meaning out of the world: God—*and man.* Of those two, however, only man can sensibly be faulted. For if the confusions of history are God's doing—if God raised up meaning on a Friday and kicked the stuffing out of it a week later, smiling an unruffled inscrutable smile all the time, then meaning simply has no meaning. Shape is nice, and so is shapelessness; gardens are nice and so are tangles, and life is nice and so is death; and history is non-history and good is evil; and nobody is to blame for anything, and away we go into the great Oriental Nothing, or All, or Whatever that doesn't give a damn. I don't know about you, but I can't buy that. It doesn't sound like much of a God to me; and it certainly doesn't sound like the God of Abraham, Isaac and Jacob.

Accordingly, the biblical insistence on blaming man for the shipwreck of history is a stroke of historical genius. It is the only way of accounting for unmeaning without having meaning fly straight out the window. And, yet, modern theologians rattle blithely on about how the story of the fall of Adam is just a historicized version of a non-historical truth (which, since this is just a plain old historical world, is simply a six-bit way of saying that it was never really true at all). But that breaks all the warps in the web right on the spot. For if, from the minute man showed up, things were the way they are now—if Adam has always been the kind of creature that wrecks the shape of the world faster than he forms it—then three unpleasant consequences are inevitable. First: the mess is God's fault, not man's. Second: it is, to say the least, disingenuous of God to go around throwing him out of gardens as a punishment for not avoiding the unavoidable. And third: it is a little surprising that man still thinks shape is better than shapelessness. If it is such a toss-up between meaning and unmeaning, why does he go on feeling that it's a bad idea to burn libraries?

What makes the theologians go on so? Something quite simple: they have been frightened by their own prehistoric men. Their heads are so full of missing links, flesh-eating apes and caveloads of cracked skulls that there is no room for the real tools of their trade. They will not touch the crucial, history-saving, theological concept. The only thing that can keep meaning from destruction by sin is a doctrine of original righteousness—some insistence that for a time at least (however short), in some place (however small), man (Adam) was good and not bad. If history never had a real chance, then there is no real history. Meaning cannot arrive late; either it comes for the first course or it does not make the party at all.

The author of the book of Genesis, therefore, is not to be sneezed at. He was a theologian who knew his trade. He provided a real beginning for the web, and he provided a way of distinguishing the building of it from the rending of it. He may need a little scientific updating now, but until someone comes along who can match him for historical sense, I hope you will excuse my not jumping on any of the bandwagons I have seen so far.

And having said that, I have done. Here endeth the longish line.

VI The Oblation of Things

I SHALL tell you now why I made that detour. I am going to talk about man's oblation of things; and in doing so, I am going to try to distinguish right oblations from wrong oblations in terms of history. I have a notion, for example, that good art is historical: a lifting, if you will, of genuine things into genuine history; and conversely, that bad art is non-historical: a lifting of fake things into non-history. But in order to make that distinction work, I had to posit it as valid for every man who ever lived—for T. S. Eliot, J. S. Bach, Michelangelo and Giotto, for Smith, Jones, Pincus and Casey, for the fellow who did the drawings of bison in the old French caves, and finally for Adam himself, whoever he was and whatever he did. Nobody can be left out. Even a single truly *prehistoric man* will wreck the whole tissue of history.

For if we are not all in the same game, there is no point in making much of the way you and I happen to be playing it now. We are just members of a crowd of discrete individuals, each of whom is only following his own nose and achieving, at best, his own amusement. If, however, we are all together in the oblation, then it becomes something more than amusement—it becomes *culture*. Drawing, music and poetry become not simply private diversions, but cities in themselves, joint ventures in the offering of specific kinds of oblations. And if that is true, our habitual assumptions about art are justified: culture exists, standards are possible, and good and bad are not meaningless noises. To put it all tightly: if Adam was truly prehistoric, culture is only a fad, a Johnny-come-lately in the history of the race. But if culture is not a fad, then Adam cannot be prehistoric; he must be right in the act with the rest of us.

On, then, with the act. Here beginneth art, culture, and the oblation of things.

ॐ

I take my children to the beach. On the north shore of Long Island it is a pretty stony proposition. The mills of the gods grind coarsely here; but, in exchange for bruised feet and a sore coccyx, they provide gravel for the foundation of the arts. Every year we hunt for perfect stones: ovals, spheroids, lozenges, eggs. By the end of the summer there are pebbles all over the house. They have no apparent use other than the delight that they provide to man, but that is the whole point of the collection. The very act of hunting them is an introduction to the oblation of things. Look at this one! Do you think it will split evenly enough for arrowheads? What color is that one when it's wet? Lick it and see. Daddy wants a big flat round one to hold the sauerkraut under the brine. Will this one do? We walk down the beach lifting stones into our history: we are collectors, ingatherers of being. Man is the lover of textures, colors and shapes—the only creature in the whole world who knows a good pickling stone when he sees one. The arts go way beyond that; but that is where they begin.

The child who runs the satin binding of his blanket between his fingers, the boy who carefully oils his collection of ball bearings so they will not rust, the woman who loves to handle thick braids, the man who opens his pocket-knife just to hear the satisfying click with which it closes— all these are priestly builders. It is in his simplest oblations that man is at his historical best. When he rises higher, he makes more mistakes—he diagrams and spiritualizes what should have been loved and offered as a thing; but at these low levels he is a success. The world has seen few badly offered blanket bindings, few profaned ball bearings. As long as man can hunt stones, he will know that the fire of his priesthood has not gone out.

But the oblation of things goes far beyond such simplicities. It is in the arts and the crafts that man most displays his priestliness and historicity. It is in them that Adam proceeds to successes and failures so vast as to defy comprehension; and it is precisely in the attempt to see them as priestly and historical that they are best understood.

It is a common error to suppose that the artist does what he does for himself—that he is a peculiar being who loves certain things in a way not open to others. It is also common to dismiss the craftsman as a fellow who does things for money. To some degree, of course, that is all true. Artists are usually a little odd; the laborer commonly, and legitimately, looks forward to his hire. But after that it falls short. For each is engaged in an offering of things not simply for his own benefit, but for the sake of the things themselves—and for the sake of other men. The painter paints because he loves the way things look and wants to offer his sight of them to others. The poet speaks because he loves words and longs for them to be heard as he hears them. And the cabinetmaker fashions and the joiner joins, and the chef cooks and the vintner toils because they love the conjunctions of things and will them to be moved into the weaving of the web. All arts come from having open eyes; and all arts are performing arts. Even the solitary artist in the cave draws to be seen, offers up what he looks at as a priest for other men. It is only in bad drawing, bad writing and bad woodwork that motives other than priestly ones become primary. It is when man stops loving what he does and stops caring whether others see that he becomes guilty of artistry that is not art and of craftsmanship that is only shoddy.

I shall give you some instances. I must choose them, of course, from such arts and crafts as I myself possess. They will have all the drawbacks of my own limited and imperfect oblation, but, if they have even a crude integrity about them, they will do for illustrations. I give you language, music and cooking.

❧

If speech is the crowning gift of man, then the arts of language probably qualify as the most nearly universal. Not all men can draw, many men cannot sing, and the world is full of cooks who ought to be allowed to rise no higher than the scullery; but all men speak, and practically no one is immune to the delights of rhyme and reason. The child, as soon as he learns words, *plays* with words. The teen-ager, with his stock of current clichés and his mercurial pattern of jargon, is a poet. He may recite only commercial slogans and comparable idiocies; but he recites them, at least partly, because he loves the way the words rattle. And somewhere along the line he will, unless he is starved to death, come to love some very grand rattles indeed.

I remember the first time I read Shakespeare's sonnets. "Lillies that fester smell far worse than weeds" stuck in my head for weeks—not so much for its meaning as for its marvelous *wordiness*. The city of speech is old and new, and rich beyond counting.

Fortunatus:

> *Flecte ramos, arbor alta, tensa laxa viscera;*
> *Et rigor lentescat ille quem dedit nativitas;*
> *Ut superni membra regis mite tendas stipite.*

Andrewes:

A cold coming they had of it. . . . The ways deep, the weather sharp, the days short, the sun farthest off, *in solstitio brumali*, in the very dead of winter.

Eliot:

> And all shall be well and
> All manner of thing shall be well
> When the tongues of flame are in-folded

Into the crowned knot of fire
And the fire and the rose are one.*

Cummings:

All in green went my love riding . . . .

That only a few have the craft to forge such words
takes nothing off the edge of the marvel by which man
can sense the priestliness of their oblation. And it is not
only the grand and the gorgeous that qualify. The world
is full of jokesters, punsters and phrase-coiners; an endless
noonday mass of badinage and repartee is offered across
the lunch tables and water coolers of the world. The *bon
mot* is as old as history. And there is the phrase we want:
the *good word*, the word in due season, like an apple of
gold in a picture of silver. The delight of talk. A highly
placed cynic once said that speech was given to man to
conceal thought. He was, of course, wrong. But the nega-
tive of it is almost as far from the truth. Speech is no mere
tool of communication; it is a joy in itself. To bring it
into history only for communication, to teach college
courses in the art of communication, to refer antiseptically
to the press and radio as communication's media is to lift
up only the smallest corner of speech for oblation. Speech
should indeed inform, as food should indeed nourish, but
what sane man will let either subject go at that? Unfor-

---

* From "Little Gidding" in *Four Quartets* by T. S. Eliot, reprinted
by permission of Harcourt, Brace & World, Inc.

tunately, much of what passes for prose only goes to prove
that sanity is in short supply.

And what a crime it is, what a sacrilege! In an age when
the word is more available than ever, the *bon mot* is harder
and harder to find. This is the era of the non-book, of the
pastiche, of the work that labors only to make a point—of
a literary spirituality that wants meaning, but will not
fondle the words which are its body. This is the era of talks,
of reports, of analyses that are unbearable because the
talkers and the writers are insufferably bad lovers. And,
to throw a stone at my own trade, it is the era of sermons
—the words of the Word!—that have no taste at all, because the preachers do not see that words themselves are
lovely.

Nothing has brought us to such poverty except the
neglect of our own priesthood. Even television cannot be
blamed. It was a brilliant device. It might have been one
of the chief builders of the city of speech. That it has
spewed forth only slogans and jingles—that it has, by and
large, not only failed to lift speech, but profaned the
language as well—is due not to its nature, but to its use
in unpriestly and unhistorical ways. It is the triumph of art
as diversion as opposed to art as oblation. Week after
week, at the cost of vast sums and heroic efforts, hopeless
plots are served up with featureless characters stuck into
them like so many raisins in a pudding. At their best they
sometimes manage to make a *point*, but they seldom reach
delight—and they threaten constantly to become pointless
altogether. To aim at communication is to aim too low. It
is the old story that, if you will not try for the best, you

will lose even the mediocre. Adam the priest cannot say the Mass of language for any other reason than the oblation of language. It will not allow itself to be used. If it is not offered, it will be lost.

ॐ

And then there is music. Men sing and drum and stamp their feet. Children chant by nature. Nobody can resist shouting into a barrel. We are mad about sound. Even the dreadful, bleating records my teen-agers listen to are minor priestly delights. The pounding beat, the socking repetitions of the tonic-subdominant chord progression—all the things they will someday come to look upon as vulgarities—are not as bad as all that. They should indeed be urged to pass beyond them, but they are nonetheless their first lessons in the seminary of sound. Left to their own devices and given a chance to play—almost anything—they are on their way to a real love of music. Think of what is in store for them. The delight of the discovery that the progression I-ii has a flavor that I-IV cannot match—that the F chord with a d in it lifts the guitar and themselves and the song into another dimension. And Tchaikowsky. I have not deliberately listened to him for ages, but there was a time when I thought that the *Fifth Symphony* was the height of music. And from there, where will it not go? My own children's tastes used to give me pause. I felt that uplift should be the order of the day. But I was wrong. They listen to trash, but it doesn't bother me anymore. If, on even a single evening of the year, just one of them will

put scratches in Uncle Hobart's record of Julian Bream—
if they wear out, in the course of their stay with me, only
the oboe solo in the Brahms *D Major Violin Concerto*—the
musical priesthood of Adam is safe for at least another
generation.

Safe, but hardly triumphant. For man's failure in music
is like his failure in all the arts—a failure to make them
really priestly, a penchant for non-historical and irrelevant
forms. Far too much of the music we now have is only
heard, not played or sung. It makes no demands, does not
ask to be lifted; it just hangs around. We have canned
music, background music, and music to do everything but
listen to music by. But music cannot be only entertainment
any more than speech can be only communication. We
aim too low. Both are major oblations, and they will
settle for nothing less. Neither can be merely used: they
must be *played*.

Thank God for wine. Without it we would have almost
no singing at all. Practically the only place where men now
sing when they are cold sober is in church; and, to tell the
truth, it sounds like it. As a professional religionist, I wish
I could make a more glowing report; but, by and large,
it is wretched. It is a triumph of use, not play. And for
every man in church who sings, there are five who stand
aloof from the whole business as if it were faintly disreputable.

Why? Because they are embarrassed by the sound of
their own voices: they are ashamed of their priesthood.
The city of music, which fairly cries for lifting into their
history, is firmly and permanently locked out. I think that

secretly, in their heart of hearts, perhaps, they envy people who play. But they do not show it often. If only they would. It isn't a matter of working themselves into miniature Isaac Sterns; the harmonica will do if it comes to that —or even tenth-rate four-part harmony. They underestimate the power of the arts. A man can practice for weeks on the strength of one-chord progression. Even the smallest oblation will lift the priest as he makes it; even a little attention to what is really there will be a historical triumph.

ॐ

Lastly, take food and the art of cooking. Once again it is a matter of the priestly lifting of things into history, a preoccupation with what really *is*. Consider the egg.

Set aside at once, for oblation at another time, all the biological and physiological marvels of it. Forget for the moment the fantastic intricacy of the mechanism from which all the higher forms of life spring. Disregard too, the wonder of its parts, its divisions, and its tremendous *complications*. Omit, finally, all other eggs but one: no frogs' eggs, ducks' eggs, robins' eggs or goose eggs; no snake eggs, no dinosaur eggs, no platypus eggs, no roe; no *ova* of any sort or kind but the eggs of the common hen. And what have you done? You have renounced a whole world only to gain a dozen in its place.

For in his priestly attention to the fruit of the barnyard —by his lifting of the egg into history—man has discovered what no other animal will ever know. What will the egg not do? It will scramble, boil, bake or fry—or go down raw if you have the stomach—and sustain and delight a man in the bargain. And that is only the start of the prologue of the introduction. It will thicken sauces, raise dough, explode into a soufflé or garnish your soup. It can be taken with sugar and whisky, or with salt and red pepper; and still you have hardly begun. Omelets are more numerous than the generations of man: Soubise, Boulestin, Paysanne or Espagnol; French, Italian, au Rhum, aux Fines Herbes; Sausage, Kidney, Lobster or Ham; and even Plain, if you like the taste of eggs. And Sauces. Mayonnaise, Hollandaise, Bearnaise and Figaro; Sabayon, Custard, Brandy and Zabaglione.

But enough. The case is closed already. What on earth is going on here if it is not the historicizing of the egg by Adam? And beyond the egg, of all foods as well. Man cooks. Oh my! how he cooks. The variety of his offerings goes so far beyond necessity, so magnificently past nourishment as to prove his priesthood without even leaving the breakfast table. Alas for cheese and wine and mushrooms! You will not make this book. Too much evidence is the mark of a weak case.

ౙ

I conclude on an adjacent note. Man eats as well as he cooks. Food enters not only the tissue of his history, but the tissue of his body, too. And sometimes it shows. He becomes a fat and well-liking priest, he acquires an amplitude that befits the dignity of his ministry. And, yet, in this silly age we insist upon making a problem of weight.

I give you, therefore, a little omnibus on Food and Fat, a *divertimento* on Dieting and History.

The root of the Hebrew word for *glory* means *weight.* In English, *girth* rhymes with *mirth* and *worth.* Everyone loves a fat man.

I remember as a child going to the beach with my uncles and my father. I can still see, glistening in the sun and surf, handsome padded expanses of *back.* I can still smell the unforgettable reek of salt, sweat and olive oil as I hung on great shoulders and rode fearlessly over the waves. But I am sure that now, if there are any such men left in the world, they are troubled about their weight—that their wives, their physicians and their friends are engaged in a vast and successful conspiracy to worry it off them.

It is the non-historical approach rampant. I remember my uncles as sacred groves, as *places* in my history, as anointed stones of the city of my being. But the diet-mongers see them only as abstract spaces. They inquire after their height—a dreadful irrelevancy to begin with —and, after consultation with a table, they arrive at what they think should be their weight. They refuse the men themselves; they insist upon a diagram of humanity instead. They dwell only upon what they would like a man to conform to; they never come within a hundred miles of knowing what a man *is.* A curse on them all! If they had their way, there would not be an uncle in all the world worth having.

Ah, you say, but surely you are not about to allow the world to be overrun by fat? Does not even a love of men for themselves—does not even a priestly and historical offering of uncles—impose some canons, some standards? Of course it does. I have nothing against reasonable efforts to remain in human shape. I object to only two things: abstract definitions of that shape, and dieting as the means of achieving it.

The abstractions are wrong because, nine times out of ten, they are based only on fads, social or medical. No chart can tell you how fat my uncles should be. You must spend some time with them before you attempt so delicate an estimate. You must see them swim and dance and carry children on their backs; you must look at them for months of Sunday-night suppers, behold them at plates of *braunschweiger* and steins of beer, before you dare to decide anything as intimate to their history as their weight.

And the dieting is wrong because it is not priestly. It is a way of using food without using it, of bringing it into your history without letting it get involved with your history. It is non-historical eating. And it is pure fraud. Bring it down to cases. Take an uncle with an embarrassingly low metabolic rate: if he gets more than 1,800 calories a day, his weight goes up out of control. He puts himself in the hands of dietary experts. They oblige him with a program. It works. At 900 calories per diem he becomes an up-to-date, low-budget uncle. But, if you see him in a year, he will have put it all back on again. And why? Because no sane human being can stand living on 1,800 calories every day till the clap of doom. So he nibbles away for a while, and then in desperation surrenders himself to creamed lobster, mashed potatoes, and a proper string of double scotches. He is lost, and he knows it. He just gives up.

The only thing that can save him is *historical* eating—eating worthy of the priesthood of Adam—eating that alternates as it should between feast and fast. The dieter is a condemned man. Every feast is, *ipso facto*, a sin. He apologizes for eating my *pâté*; he abjectly acknowledges his guilt over my wife's Cake à la Bennich. Good is evil to him, and bounty a burden. But if he would fast! If he would take *no* food on Wednesday—and none on Tuesday too, if he wills to reign like a king—what prodigies might he not perform at Thursday's dinner; how, like a giant, go from course to course?

What a poor, benighted age we live in. How we deny ourselves all sauces but the best. How little of what surrounds us is ever offered either by use or abstinence. And there is the secret. Fasting is an offering, too. The dieter says: Sweets are bad; I cannot have them ever. The faster says: Sweets are good; I will not take them now. The dieter is condemned to bitter bondage, to a life which dares not let food in. But the faster is a man preparing for a feast. His Lent leads to an Easter, and to mirth and weight of Glory.

VII The Main Thing

BETWEEN the oblation of things and the oblation of persons, there is a great gulf fixed. When I lift an egg into my history, the egg is, for all practical purposes, passive. It is content to come on my terms. To be sure, it will come on its own terms too—it will be fresh or rotten, large or small, single- or double-yolked, as it chooses—but its concern for itself is of a fairly undemanding sort. As far as history is concerned, my use of the egg is pretty much a one-way street: *it* becomes involved in my history; I do not, in any important sense, become involved in its. Indeed, on the definition of man as the historical animal, the egg does not really have any history to involve me in.

There are, of course, creatures other than man that can draw man into their works. To a dramatic extent. There are rivers in flood and there are hurricanes and tornadoes. And, if you like individual attention, there are army ants and man-eating sharks. But even in such cases man hardly sees himself as being invited into someone else's history; he feels more put upon that asked, more consumed than offered. By an exceedingly charitable stretch of the imagination, he might find some small satisfaction in the knowledge that the shark will be fatter and more well-liking for having digested him: the process *is* a part of the web. But charity

like that is rare. Commonly—and justifiably—we like our
meanings a little more meaningful. The histories involved
are so disparate that we prefer to save the name "history"
for the human side of the operation.

Man's oblation of *things*, therefore, for all its complexities, remains fairly tractable. It is his offering of *persons*
that is the really difficult work. For when he offers up other
human beings—when he invites, or is invited by, other
persons into the exchanges of the city—he steps into a
two-way street. Or an eight-lane expressway! While he
offers them, they are just as busy offering him; he receives
invitations not by return mail, but in the same post. As far
as eggs and wine and dogs and violins are concerned, I am
more or less in command of the situation. I am, within
tolerable limits, the master of my fate. But as far as John
or Harry, or *that girl with the marvelous green eyes!* are
concerned, they are just as much masters as I am. They, of
their fate, and I of mine—most likely—but all of each
other's, too; and there's the historic rub. As long as history
is only a question of how an "I" will handle an "it," the
achievement of decent—of fitting—oblations is at least
imaginable. But as soon as it becomes a matter of two "I's"
offering each other simultaneously, we have entered the
realm of outsized offerings, of oblations 9½ AAAA and
6 EEE. The salutary "I-Thou" relationship is also the
world's principal source of blisters and corns.

The job of taking two independent persons, two historic
animals—two histories—and bringing them together in love
or friendship, in marriage or business, has always been
ticklish. A man can usually manage to be clear in his mind

about what he takes to be his own meaning—his personal view of the shape of things; and most men can make reasonable allowances for the fact that other people see different meanings and different shapes. But for two such beings to undertake a *joint* meaning! To attempt to make room in *my* history for *your* history, without slighting either or wrecking both! Why, it's a wonder we even dare ask anyone the time of day, let alone think of inviting his friendship, his devotion, his love. That we so commonly do, of course, is the most convincing of all the proofs of the existence of the city—of history. That anything with such odds against it should be attempted with such unabashed regularity can only mean that we were built for nothing else. It is as if every man in the world chose daily to go over Niagara Falls in a barrel. It proves something about human nature. If an animal plays dangerously, we conclude it is built for danger; when man goes through the world with his eyes open for friendships, for alliances, for love—when he is so continually *on the make*, morally or immorally, inviting whole histories into his history—it can only mean that history is his native air.

By and by I shall have something to say about the leonine, the tigerish, the fierce and wild way in which, for ill and for good, we play the game of history with other persons. First, however, one last item from the realm of things still demands attention. It is the human body.

Trumpets, towels, tripe and teapots; razors, Rembrandts, radios and rattlesnakes; the world is full of a number of things. Isaiah, Jeremiah, Ezekiel, Daniel; Merrill Lynch, Pierce and Smith; it is more than equally full of persons.

But lying on the borderline between the two is the flesh of which man is compounded. It is a *thing*, to be sure, but in a class by itself. Pierce could be Pierce without his desk, his coat or his debentures; but without his body, he is not Pierce at all. The body is not a thing that *belongs to* us; it is something that is inseparable from us. Of all the things that can or will be involved in a man's history, his body is the foremost. As long as he is, it is. He has no choice about it.

But that does not mean he has no choices. History is precisely the conscious and voluntary oblation of the world. Accordingly, his body, of all things, must be consciously and voluntarily offered. And not only *his* body, but other men's too. His wife, his children, his friends, his collaborators, all come to him as bodies—as *things* that are, at the same time, *persons*; and as persons who are, to an alarming degree, things. Behold, therefore, a historical world—a world of uplifted grandfathers and offered uncles, and of innumerable ministers who hold each other's bodies in their priestly hands.

ॐ

One might think that the very *bodiness*—the corporality —of human nature would be proof against the grosser forms of unreality. It seems only reasonable to hope that the fact that we are *things* would keep us from wandering off into the more monumental historical irrelevancies. But it is not necessarily any more so here than it is in the arts and crafts.

As a matter of fact, it is probably safe to say that since the human body is the *main thing* in the world, it will be the subject of the principal perversions, of the most unhistoric oblations. And it is.

Take, first of all, the notion that the body is, by its very nature, evil—unworthy of, or inimical to, the real being of man. Oriental religions, of course, have made the most of that idea, but there is hardly a thinking part of the world that hasn't had an attack of it at one time or another. No doubt most modern people—misreading St. Paul on the subject of the warfare between the flesh (fallen nature) and the Spirit (God the Holy Ghost)—think that the Christian religion takes a dim view of the body in all its parts and passions. Puritanism is commonly looked upon not as a Christian heresy, which it is, but as the genuinely Christian view, which it is not by a long shot.

Set down here, therefore, the fact that orthodox Christianity has nothing against the body, and everything for it. First, God made it. Second, God loves it. Third, God took it to himself in the womb of Mary. Fourth, he walked the earth in it, not with disdain, but with enough obvious pleasure to acquire a bad reputation in the eyes of fussy people. And, finally, he died, rose, ascended into heaven, and reigns forever as the *incarnate* Lord—in a body—with *flesh, bones and all things appertaining to the perfection of man's nature.* The problems raised by orthodox Christianity are anything but Oriental. They are embarrassingly —shockingly—*fleshly.* The current age, if it hears the true doctrine at all, finds it not too spiritual, but too *material*

for its tastes. It is not God who is too refined for man. It
is man who finds God's announced way of doing business
slightly . . . vulgar.

Or take the long and peculiar history of sexual fetishes.
There are few places in the world where man has been
content to leave the glorious normality of the human
body—male or female—alone for long. Not satisfied with
offering up lips that looked like lips, or skin that looked
like skin, or feet that looked like feet . . . *tacet* the rest
. . . he has resorted to doing tricks with them. Usually,
rather sordid tricks; and, almost as often, grim, solemn,
quasi-religious tricks. Only the prurient find them entertaining: we easily see the unhistorical offerings of other
nations as unhistorical. But at home, in our own backyards,
we are not always so clear. We grow used to our fetishes;
they become second nature. One man's meat is another
man's perversion. The nearly universal penchant of the
human race for shying away from the real shape of the
body and fastening its desires on irrelevancies ought to be
a giveaway that something radically unhistorical is going on.
When the body has to be pinched, stretched or reprocessed
before we can get enthusiastic about it, there is a good case
to be made out that it is not being loved or offered *as a body*.

The history of fashions in dress fits nicely into that case.
In spite of the fact that the Scriptures mention clothes only
after the fall, I do not think that clothing can be dismissed
simply as the attempt of Adam to hide his shame. Dress is
as much an art as is cooking. If you are allowed to put
chives on top of rice, it must be equally lawful to put
lamb's wool on top of a man—provided only that you do

the job historically. Both the chives and the rice, both the wool and the man must come through the operation enhanced, lifted, *offered*. The true materialities involved must be respected, and the conjunctions between them must be appropriate. But, given that, clothing is one of the glories of man.

In heaven we shall wear white robes—no doubt something more stylish than flour sacks, too. The picture of Christ in majesty at the beginning of the Revelation of St. John the Divine is not only majestic; it has about it a hint of sartorial elegance. The golden girdle is not a necessary piece of equipment; it is a stunning and gracious touch. Clothing is with us for good; nudism, it would seem, is only another wrong turn. It is like restricting yourself to raw vegetables. The unadorned body is indeed a glorious thing, like the unadorned apple. But the man who will rob me of my pie, my strudel, my turnovers and my sauce is unhistorical and mad. I will have no truck with him. An apple vested with pastry is not less, but more, an apple. It is an apple displayed and regnant.

The arts of embellishment. Perhaps that is the phrase. Man *dresses* his meat, he *vests* his table, he *drapes* his windows—and he *clothes* his body. That the decorative arts are not as grand as the creative arts says nothing against them. They are still an oblation, and, as such, they enter the web. The idiocies of the history of tailoring must not disenchant us about the sanity of the subject itself. Bad baroque is only the failure to embellish germanely; euphuistic prose is only speech offered up without real respect for language. And foolish fashion is the same. Whatever man does often, he will also do badly, with alarming frequency; but he must not be stopped for all that.

To walk through New York City is to see everything at once, especially in the matter of clothing. Much of what meets the eye is, of course, dreadful. For every woman whose clothing is a compliment to her body, there are five who walk wrapped in insults. I offer to women, therefore, three categories—three glittering, but not entirely useless, generalities—in terms of which a woman may judge the priestliness of her own dressing: by her clothing, she may turn herself into a Frump, or a Tomato, or a *Woman*.

The Frump is the woman who, either by ignorance or choice, does not really dress at all: she simply puts things on. Poverty has nothing to do with it. You can find Frumps in the fanciest parts of the city. And you can see real women in the poorest. Dress depends, as do all the arts, on taste and craft and talent more than on resources. Money helps, but it helps only the artist. For the bungler, it only insures more stately monstrosities. The Frump might as well not have a body at all, for all the good her dressing does her. If only she would hold herself in more priestly hands!

The Tomato, on the other hand, is another breed. As far as she is concerned, her chief concern is to display her body. But alas! The clothes she selects display only her unpriestliness, her inattention to what her body really looks like. She has, poor girl, accepted the fetishes as the truth: she has poured her body into a shape it does not fit, set it upon heels on which it cannot walk, and decorated it with whatever irrelevancies happen to have caught the current fancy. She draws, no doubt, the lioness' share of looks and whistles, but only because the crowd is as blind as she is. She always makes me a little sad: I see her as living evidence of the way we waste ourselves. If she is young, I am sad because she could be so much more stunning than she is. And if she is old, she breaks my heart. At 55, Tomatoes should not be out on the stand at all.

But then there are *Women*. And New York, since it has lots of everything, has Women on practically every street. Real pieces of history moving graciously past my history as I walk! Rich and poor, old and young, tailored and casual; how they *strike*, how they *stun*, how they *ravish*! All praise to their tailors, uptown or down. And greater praise to themselves, for they have exalted their bodies and put on robes of glory. If there is a sartorial section of purgatory, they will, no doubt, pass through it in an instant, while their poor sisters have to spend ages unlearning all the things they thought they knew. Nevertheless, I judge them not. I leave all such divisions to wiser and purer eyes than mine. Here at least is one fool who will not rush in. Let Women only remember their priesthood, and vest themselves accordingly.

And men? Well, I think we will all have to do some time for the way we dress. That a man—the flower of God's creation, the Lord of the world—should walk his native land clad almost invariaby in a collection of cloth tubes hitched together with a leather thong can be tolerable only to a people who have clean forgotten what a man's body looks like. What have we done to ourselves? Where was it we forgot that a man's legs alone are so delightful that the psalmist felt obliged to insist the Lord is not influenced by them? Why no kilts, no hose? Or if you like concealment and majesty in your decoration, why no togas, no robes? Go and stand at the U.N. Watch an African chieftain glide by. Then walk through Brooks Brothers, if you dare.

As a priest, I have a privilege reserved to only a few in this dull age. Along with judges and academic dignitaries, I wear meaningful robes. It is an enviable distinction. And the envy can be felt. Most men will gladly put on a cassock, if only they can manage to set aside what the world has so foolishly taught them about skirts. And they will even more gladly put on a real cloak.

While not actually a vestment, the heavy black melton cloak is a standard item of the priest's wardrobe. When properly made, it is a vast semicircular garment, reaching from shoulder to heel and capable of keeping out any wind that ever blew. The ordinary name for it is a "cemetery cloak," after the most notable place of its use. The vestment houses, however, sensing that they are dealing with greatness, give it a grander name: *Cappa Nigra* or *Cappa Magna*; and they frequently give it a deep hood to crown the mystery. If you hand it to an ordinary man and tell him to put it on, he will always hesitate. It is like the marsh reed: it threatens to make too much of him. But let him wear it once, and you may have a candidate for Orders on your hands. Humankind cannot stand very much reality; but it loves the smell of it just the same.

༜

Clothes, however, vest only the least part of the body. The seven-eighths of man from the neck down are no match for the crown which sits above it: his *face*. For it is in the face that the body most clearly ceases to *belong to* a man, and *becomes* the man himself. Face is the physical counterpart of *name*, and both are easy synonyms for *person*: if my name *and* my face are forgotten, I am nobody indeed. It is, therefore, the oblation of face—the using, the shaping, the adornment of the countenance of man—that, of all physical offerings, lies nearest to the lifting of persons into history. If man's body is the *main thing*, then his face must be the mainmost—thing of thing, image of image, very thing of very thing.

And the subway is the place to behold it, to see the glory of it when offered historically—or to feel it escape you completely when it is not. Look at the women! A real face is worth all the weeks of waiting you have to go through to find it. At any age—and in an incredible variety of shapes—it speaks, and is heard, as a précis of history: *There goes somebody!* The offering is rich beyond measure. But it is also rare. There is a frump face to go with slatternly clothes, and there is a tomato face to match the tomato suit. Make-up is indeed allowable—even an art. But, in the hands of such women, faces are not made up—they are made down, made over, belittled, *unmade*. They take the most personal thing in the world, the ultimate sacrament of uniqueness, and recast is as the millionth extrusion of a common mold. Though it is worn by fifty women, it makes no difference between them. They are not persons, they are a class; and a retarded class at that.

Their hair is set with no respect to their faces. Their eyebrows are applied at random, like incomprehensible italics. Their lips are irrelevant parentheses, wrecking the very context they were designed to clarify. Behind the make-up, there is indeed something personal and singular, but it has all but slipped away through unpriestly oblation. Faces? Hardly. Defacings. Estranged faces! The women who wear them are so far from looking like anybody in particular that only a man as far removed from reality as they are could possibly behold them gladly. Unfortunately for us all, however, there are plenty of both, and the pointless masque goes on and on. A woman's face is a rare thing.

To the credit of men, the same cannot fairly be said of them. The subway teems with individuals. There is nothing in the world like the unadorned variety of men's faces. It is entirely possible to make out an airtight case for the reality of history from their noses alone. That anything so modest should be capable of such *effect*—and that such minor changes in it should so transform an entire countenance—can only mean that the primary function of the nose is to *mean*, to signify, to declare. Smelling is merely a faculty which occupies a closet somewhere inside the head; it is the nose itself that is . . . well, everything Cyrano said it was, and then some.

And if, on top of that, you receive into evidence the rest of the wonder of men's faces—the diversity of their outlines (long and thin, round and beaming, squarish, oval, even, odd), the multitude of their jaws (Lantern, Milquetoast, English Bull), and the endless peculiarities of their eyes, their ears, their hairlines and their cheekbones—you drown yourself in an ocean of proof for personality. Faces are the chiefest things of history. One man's face by itself is a whole sea of matter, uplifted, and for oblation; a single subway car contains the raw materials of a universe of men, every one of whom will be an uncle worthy of offering. And were you to take a trainful, a stationload . . .

LECTOR: Ahem!

AUCTOR: Yes?

LECTOR: I wonder if I might ask you a personal question.

AUCTOR: Yes?

LECTOR: Your own face. It is . . . . . well, half-hidden behind your beard.

AUCTOR: Yes?

LECTOR: Am I to assume that you find this consistent with a historical oblation of faces?

AUCTOR: You are.

LECTOR: I have a feeling you are avoiding the issue.

AUCTOR: I am.

LECTOR: This is not at all like you. Why will you not speak out? Why not say plainly how beards are historical?

AUCTOR: I was trying to spare you. The Beard is even more meaningful than the nose—its historicity would require volumes to do it justice.

LECTOR: Can you not possibly be brief?

AUCTOR: You are like all the others. You are unworthy of

even an outline of the outline. But you have piqued me. I shall speak.

To the question, Why do you have a beard?, seventeen answers are possible. They are as follows:

(Simple): I like it.

(Taciturn): I just do.

(Sheepish): Lots of men have beards.

(Rude): None of your business.

(Cowardly): Oh? Don't you like it?

(Confident): It is manly.

(Overconfident): It keeps women away.

(Practical, *in respectu causae efficientis*): Because I don't shave.

(Agnostic): I don't know; I stopped shaving and it grew.

(Theological, but cautious): You will have to ask God.

(Practical, *propter incommoditatem rasurarum*): I was tired of cutting myself every morning.

(Devout): It is a gift of God.

(Practical, *pro bono prolis*): I look more paternal with one.

(Meditative): It would be ungrateful to die without having seen it.

(Practical, *sed propter vanitatem*): It hides my weak chin.

(Theological, *propter causam finalem*): God meant man to have one.

(Practical, *pro placenda uxore*): It tickles my wife.

In deference to your impatience, I now skip whole tractates—their titles, in part: Of the Colors of Beards; Of the Shapes of Beards; Of the Lawfulness of Trimming Beards; Of the Optimum Length of Beards; Of the Classes of Men Who May Rightly Choose to Go Beardless;—and out of the whole of the *magnum opus* I give you only a digest of the abstract of the XIV Tractate: Of the Historicity and Priestliness of Beards.

History is the shape of change; and change, to be noticeable, must be neither too fast nor too slow. A man's face, however, principal though it may be among the things of the world, sacrament of history though it is, does not, for the most part, change at a *convenient* pace: its smiles and winks are too fleeting for record, and its growth and aging too slow for continuous attention. What is needed is something that will move slowly enough so that its motion will go unnoticed, but still change quickly enough to constitute a daily or weekly reminder of history. God, therefore, to give man a perpetual memorial of the fact that his changing must be shaped—that his face must make history—gave him *hair*. To women, hair upon the crown, to grow long with the addition of days, and to require shaping and formation. And to men, hair upon cheek and jowl, hair to lend suitable majesty to the oracle of his mouth, so that even the greatest fool might swear by the beard of the prophet.

For most of the animals, God provided only *reasonable* tegument, hair that grew to a convenient length and then stopped, hair that needed no historicizing. But the hair he gave to man was a gift *in excess*, a deliberate inconvenience, an awkwardness that could become majestic only by oblation. The choicest ages of the world have been precisely those in which man's hair has been offered historically. And, conversely, the most benighted ages have been the eras in which the razor has been rampant. A short beard, a curled beard, a braided beard, even—if it must be—a moustache, is hair historicized. But a clean-shaven face is hair obliterated. It is evidence not of oblation, but of history washed down the sink. What might have been a daily offering is only a loss; the morning sacrifice of man turns out to be only a murder.

ℰ

But enough. I give you no more. You have served to bring me to an end. Man's body, lovely in eyes and lovely in limbs, cries for oblation. Even a light lifting of it lifts the priest as he offers. No thing, let alone the main thing, is evil: *Ens inquantum ens est bonum.* The body is not the solemn burden that we have made it, not the grim totem the world takes it to be: it is a noble animal, a fabulous steed, whom God has appointed to keep us company and to bear us home. Brother Ass was made to carry the king into history. What a pity we do not show the beast more love.

VIII The Courting Dance

WHEN it comes to the oblation of persons, there is a loose but tempting connection waiting to be picked up. In English, the words *person, parson* and *priest* are near neighbors: they share some footage of fence in the backyard of usage. Enough, at any rate, to suggest that somebody has already caught the hint that both parson and person are up to the same thing—that both are priests, offerers. The definition of man as a person, and of person as a priestly agent within history, turns out to be not altogether whimsical.

But for all that, it still does not turn out to be the common one. We assume, of course, that it is. We take it for granted that the concept of person is so firmly built into our philosophies and institutions that we hardly need give it a thought. Yet, for the past hundred years or so, it has had a hard time maintaining itself. Most modern definitions of man are non-personal or impersonal. At their best, they ignore the concept; at their worst, they positively destroy it. It is another case of illegible legends. I shall not spend any more time on them than it takes to note what is perhaps their principal feature: a penchant for the words *only* and *nothing but.*

Man, we are told, is *only* the product of biological evolution. A human being, the announcements proclaim, is *simply* so many dollars worth of elements. Thought, they insist, is *nothing but* electro-magnetic impulses in the brain. There is a name for this line of argument. It is called the reductionist fallacy. It takes something that is a complex whole and defines it only in terms of its parts. It reduces what a thing *is* to what a thing is *made of*. It will allow only operational, not metaphysical definitions.

For example. A bio-medical engineer, in the course of his experiments, comes up with some amazing facts. He finds that the electrical stimulation of certain centers of the brain, or the minute adjustment of certain aspects of body chemistry, will produce the subjective sensation of, say, stark terror, complete serenity, or philosophical omnicompetence. It is a remarkable discovery; and it is one in which any man can take legitimate intellectual delight. To know anything real is indeed good. Unfortunately, however, the engineer usually goes a step further. Not content with having arrived at positive knowledge, he feels compelled to insist that his physical discoveries are the only valid positive knowledge available. As a result, he comes up with a statement that catapults him abruptly out of the physical and into the metaphysical realm. He proclaims that terror, serenity, or philosophy are nothing but physical phenomena. He becomes a reductionist. For him, the fact that young love and mild indigestion use the same physical equipment constitutes an all but overwhelming temptation to refuse to see any real difference between them.

If he would confine himself to his own physical researches, it is quite possible that he might do some good

—at least as far as advancing knowledge within his own field is concerned. But when he turns himself loose in law or politics, in love or marriage, he becomes a menace. He will quickly insist, of course, that he intends only to speak about physical reality; he will usually disown any metaphysical designs. But the disclaimer comes too late. The minute a man employs the reductionist argument, he is already waist-deep in metaphysics, with the water rising around him like a river in flood. For what he has really said is that metaphysics is either an impossibility or a merely subjective exercise. In any case, he has reached the dangerous point of having gone to work on metaphysical concepts without a single truly metaphysical tool in his kit.

That is why the concept of person has to be kept alive. In an age when all kinds of experts are more than ready to tell us that only our parts really count, we need to retain a firm grip on the notion that the whole man is what matters; that a man's *name*, his identity as a person —who he is as distinct from what he is—is the most important thing about him. We need a metaphysical grasp of man. The law, of course, and politics as practiced in a democracy, still act as if the metaphysical notion of person were the key concept in anthropology. But most lawyers and politicians have long since fallen short of it. They have, along with the rest of us, been sold a merely physical—an engineering—view of human nature. Man, in their hands, is always imminently in danger of being used, operated, manipulated rather than respected.

To illustrate. From time to time, the question of euthanasia manages to become one of the features of the press. It is argued that if a man, by accident of fate or birth, has reached the state at which he is "only a vegetable," we should be allowed, quietly and painlessly, to dispatch him from life. The contention is that so much of his equipment is gone that he no longer qualifies as human anyway. The law, of course, will have no truck with this. It goes right on treating him as a person and insisting that nobody has a right to do him in. But the euthanasia enthusiasts are quite ready to lobby for a change. God help us all if they succeed.

The flaw in their argument lies under that little qualifier about guaranteeing the painlessness of the *coup de grâce.* They seem always to feel obliged to pretty it up. But, on their reasoning, that is totally unnecessary. It is only a sop thrown to the human consensus they are about to evict from the halls of justice. If the poor "basket case" (even their words are impersonal and grim) is no longer human, why don't they simply add some cement blocks to the basket and drown him like a cat? Why the expense, why the ritual of disposing of him as if he still mattered?

The answer, of course, is that even in abolishing the notion of person, they can never cut all of their ties with it. They will, when the time comes, duly bury their own dead. Aunt Suzie's body, even after it is less than a vegetable, will be ceremoniously laid away. And, after the funeral, they will—destroying their whole case in the process—go and sit in a lawyer's office for the reading of a piece of paper that will inform them, the living, of the present, and sometimes devastatingly effective, *Will* of the deceased. The law not only treats Aunt Suzie as a person in life; it allows her to go on making history after death.

I propose, therefore, to ignore the engineers and their enthusiasms. But I also propose that, at the same time, we all keep one eye very carefully glued on them. Some day, no doubt, they will reach such heights of refinement that they will be able to duplicate all of the physical components of man; and the day after that they will probably find a way of pasting them together so that they will be able to announce triumphantly that they have manufactured a human being. When that time comes, we must all be ready to explain patiently to them that they have done no such thing. We must tell them that they have only foolishly succeeded in conferring real being on something which the race, so far, has been wise enough to confine to fairy tales. They will have made a Troll, a Goblin, an Orc. They will have brought forth to the light of day something which can *do* everything a man does without being what a man *is*. They will have made an *it*, not a *person*. And if they insist, as they will, on bringing it to tea or to Mass, let us hope and pray that somewhere in Christendom there will still be a bishop wise enough to instruct the faithful to throw stones at it, *ad majorem Dei gloriam*.

Out, then, with the reductionists and their trolls! And up with man the person—with history's parson, meaning's priest. We have neglected him far too long already. There are vast technologies waiting anxiously in the wings. Unless we are ready with a clear defense of person, we shall all be shoved offstage by the goblins. Remember I told you so. *Hora novissima, tempora pessima sunt, vigilemus!*

℘

To work then. The first thing to be insisted upon is the fact that every personal offering of history must be precisely a priestly one. It is not enough simply to obtrude histories upon one another.

We affect those around us in many ways. Because history is a shaping, a selection, of the events that chronicle hands us, history necessarily involves chronicle. Accordingly, if I can manage to intrude, by main force or stupidity, into somebody else's chronicle, I will, to some degree at least, have become a possible candidate for inclusion in his history. If my car crumples my neighbor's fender, if my dog chases his cat, if my fist lands in his face, we are already on the edge of affecting each other's histories. If he is a wise man, of course, he will certainly ignore the first two, and probably ignore the third; but wise men are rare: an incredible amount of meaning is commonly read into such events. And if I go further—if I water his stock, foreclose his mortgage or slander his name—well, I am in his history almost willy-nilly. We are, by one leap, in a position to make or break each other.

Whether two persons come together in an oblation that makes history, however, will depend on more than common chronicle. It will depend not only on what they do *to* each other, but on what they do *with* each other—on the priestly or unpriestly offerings they make of what has happened. And that means that no truly personal relationship can be left to fend for itself. It must be seen, in advance, as an imminent oblation, and it must be shaped accordingly. The approach of man to man is precisely a dance, and a courting dance at that. None of my meetings with another man is a mere event, either in his life or mine. Every introduction is an invitation into each other's meaning, a *terrible* opening of one history to another. In friendship, love or alliance we enter inexorable exchanges, rendering death and forever at each breathing.

Needless to say, we do not commonly see the kind of care we should expect in such meetings. Even in the most deliberate invitations—when we invite love, when we propose marriage—we act frighteningly off the cuff. We come at each other as casually as we approach watermelons. We hold each other in careless, calloused hands. We see those we should offer only as beings to be used. We grasp them, but we watch ourselves.

One of the appalling aspects of the pastoral ministry is the gradual discovery of how badly man deals with other men. Wives, husbands, parents, children—so many of them are only handled, not offered. Yet, even in the worst cases there was always a time at which the note of *courtship*—of gracious invitation, of courteous oblation—was not only present, but predominant. The utterly broken marriage, the relationship in which the partners can now see nothing but misused advantage, was once a priestly thing in which they gave themselves as each other's ministers.

That is the first key to the mystery of courtship. I do not want at this point to narrow the notion too much.

Romantic love will come in soon enough. Here I want only to use the word to describe the inveterate desire we conceive, at certain times and toward certain persons, to open ourselves to them and to invite them into our history. I want to keep its definition broad enough to include not only the approach of man to maid, but also the motion of Smith toward the fellow on the next barstool or of a clerk in bookkeeping toward a typist in public relations.

Why do we do it at all, when we so commonly do it badly? Why this perpetual mating ritual in such a monumentally frustrating world? What does it mean, except that we were built for courting, for courtesy, and that, God help us, we can do no other. But if that is true, then our real work becomes at least a little clearer. It is not to find a way around the courting, but to find a way through it. Not to avoid it, but to understand it and to try to see that we do it courteously, personally, in ways worthy of the priesthood of man.

When I take up with someone else (the phrase is solid, and priestly, too), I enter into a transaction which, if it does not involve oblation, will necessarily mean disaster. When I behold a dog or offer a cat, I must take care that I behold it for *itself*, not just for *myself*. Even things cannot simply be used. But when I behold Henry or Mary, I step off the deep end of oblation; for I am inviting into my history beings that cannot—that will not—allow themselves to be used. Unless I undertake to lift them for themselves, they will begin to snarl at my concern; unless my invitation evokes an invitation in return, we are in for trouble.

For themselves. The ultimate mystery of personality—of personhood—is that no person exists for his own sake. As a matter of fact, it is precisely my own welfare that is the last thing in the world I am to be concerned with. The priest is to spend his days offering for others: the Good Shepherd giveth his life for the sheep. The beholding, the loving—the adoration, if you will—of my own being is somebody else's business, not mine. Persons were meant to enter into a dance of mutual oblation, a simultaneous offering of each other. The city, the web, history itself, is the tissue woven by such priestly acts. That it has not been built well in this fallen world goes to prove only that the world is indeed fallen—that the exchanges which were ordained to weave the web are the very ones which, by perversion, have been its destruction. But in all the long and disastrous history of his courting, Adam has never ceased to court. The only trouble is that he courts himself first. Pride, self-love, egotism, are only—are precisely—the right oblation offered by the wrong priest. Like all classic perversions, they are just a whisker away from the truth.

We were meant, therefore, to do easily and courteously for each other what we must under no circumstances attempt to do for ourselves. Narcissus perished for looking at himself; had he done exactly the same thing for another, he would have thrived. The mirror is a tricky proposition. A priest, when he goes to say Mass, puts on his vestments in a side room. Every proper sacristy has a mirror, often a full-length one. So far so good. There is no excuse for slovenliness at the altar of God; anything that will help the priest go to the sanctuary properly hitched and neatly girded is a help. But I think that most priests have some misgivings about their sacristy mirrors. A man who is about to offer up all things in loving adoration perceives the impropriety of spending even a second looking at himself. It is disconcerting; it is imminently . . . perverse. I always feel better when it is an altar boy or a fellow priest who casts the final approving glance at the gathering of my alb or the set of my chasuble.

Our fellow priests. There is the word. The offerers who make sacred for us what we ourselves would only profane. And how we need them! How we cry day and night for those priestly others who will love our faces, our bodies, and the marvelously odd twists of our minds! Not, God forbid, so we can be appreciated, accepted, or gratified. Not for any of the dreadful psychological reasons for which the world tells us we need them. But in order that we can be delivered from the horrible burden of trying to appreciate ourselves—so we can be about the business of saying our own Mass for somebody else, free in the knowledge that others have already taken care of us. Self-preservation may be the law of the jungle, but only mutual and priestly oblation can build the city.

❦

Courting *in genere*, however—courting in the wide sense, as the priestly invitation of all other persons for offering, holds only a small candle to courting *in specie* —courting as the way of men and women with each other.

The first is a loose and general diagram of the oblation; the second is the rich and detailed picture. It goes no better than the former, of course; indeed, it goes worse: it is an invitation to more intricate involvements and to vastly greater inexorabilities. But it goes—and goes and goes—just the same.

Nowhere else is the priestly approach to other persons quite so clearly drawn as in the first motions of courtly, of romantic, love. The whole desire of the *courteous* lover is to sing the praises of the beloved and to hold her up for adoration. It is precisely the priesthood of man that is the root of romance; not sexual desire or rational analysis. They come in soon enough, of course, but in the first instance they are palpable irrelevancies. They may well be the cause of eighty per cent of the affairs in the world, and of one hundred per cent of the hanky-panky: sex and logic are indeed heady draughts. But the recognizable rightness of the romantic oblation remains the overpowering elixir. It is the *courtliness* of the offering of the beloved that intoxicates: the joy, the ease, the elation with which we become each other's ministers is the straight 100-proof marvel.

But there is more. The priesthood of Adam is the instrument of meaning as well as the spring of joy; romantic love makes history just as necessarily as it sings praises. How well do you remember? There is a small and entirely common English word which will prove it to you. You used it all your life—easily, almost meaninglessly. If someone asked you, as a child, to select the ten most thrilling words in the world, you would not have thought of this

one in a million tries. And yet there was a day—when? at
sixteen? at eighteen?—on which it became the bearer of an
overwhelming freight of joy. You stood next to someone
with whom you had entered into mutual oblation, and in
the casual utterance of it you came face to face with an
unexpected burst of meaning. One or the other of you
spoke the blessed word: *us*.

History is made in moments, in decisive instants of transition. And the creation of an *us* from what was only an *I*
and a *thou* is one of them. Nothing is a clearer proof of the
historical nature of man than the thrill of meaning, of
shape—of history—which invariably accompanies it. Even
if it is forgotten forever ten minutes after it was spoken,
the mere occurrence of it remains a monumental giveaway
that history is our meat—that the achievement of meaning,
the weaving of the web, is the real reason for our ceaseless
courting of one another. If we came together only to use,
or to gratify—if we met only to blow hot-breathed I-need-
you's or greedy I-want-you's at each other—no little word
like *us* could matter the way it does. If our courting were
only flirtation—only a dabbling with history, only a toying
with persons—the discovery that *I* have suddenly become
involved in *us* would be a nuisance, not a thrill.

Indeed, unless our courting is deliberately pursued as
historic, it will be not only a nuisance, but a menace. There
is no middle ground between use and oblation. Once the
word *us* has been uttered, a new and common history has
been created by fiat of adoration. It can make us or break
us, but there is no easy turning from it. It is precisely the
new historical entity *we* that must now become not only

a new object for oblation, but a priestly agent in its own right. As I and Thou became *we* by mutual oblation, so *we* now must walk into history to make a joint offering of other things and other persons.

Oblations multiply. John Smith courts Mary Jones. He becomes her lover, her offerer, her priest. Courteously, she returns the oblation and obliges him with her love. Two priests; two oblations. But now they are John-and-Mary—the Smiths—and that makes a third priest who must offer and a third history which must be lifted up. Where does it stop? It doesn't. John must now offer *us*, and *we* must offer John; and John-and-Mary together must become the offerers of the Davises next door and of all the intractable in-laws and relatives who present themselves for oblation. All this, mind you, and they have hardly even begun to offer. Allow them, in addition, only a modest number of children and only the few years it takes for the children they beget and the family they constitute to become priestly agents themselves—and what have you? A web? A tissue? The words are too poor. You have a brocade, a tapestry of mutual oblation. Even in one small corner of the world, the shuttles fly so fast and the warps come so thick upon each other that the mind staggers to comprehend the weaving.

And if the making of history is so, how complex, how snarled, how tangled beyond all possibility of grasp or unravelling must be the unmaking, the failure to offer. The loom on which we weave cannot be stopped short: it produces triumphs or disasters, but nothing in between. *Corruptio optimi pessima.* Lilies that fester smell far worse than weeds. If, with our friends, we allow use to replace oblation; if into our marriages we admit competitive, exclusive oblations; if toward our children we extend only surly tolerance where there should be priestly lifting, what wreckage must we not expect? The really appalling thing about us is that we are so regularly appalled by the way things go wrong. If we knew our nature and our failings better, there would be much less room for surprise and perhaps a little more seriousness about the necessity of oblation all across the board.

For if no *single* priestly agent can safely act for himself —if every individual man must say his Mass for another, lest he perish by pride—then the same is true of a compound priestly agent, of an I and a Thou who by mutual oblation have made themselves an *us*. They entered a common history by opening their eyes upon each other and by lifting each other in love. But now that they are in it, they must take care to act in their new priesthood: to look out, not in; to offer not themselves, but others. Friend and friend, man and wife, enter a joint—a *collegial*—priesthood. If they insist upon looking only at themselves, if they think that the meaning of their romantic meeting can be saved by celebrating only the original and private rituals of courtship, they will wreck everything. When a friendship or a marriage degenerates into a discussion of what it means to the individuals involved, it is already lost. We cannot safely look at each other beyond the initial courting. I and thou must, to a large degree, be replaced by *us*; we must stand in our new history, not facing each other, but side by side. Courtship is the invitation, not to a life of private Masses, but to a joint Mass in a new and common priesthood—to a concelebration, if you please—for the lifting up of all that is not ourselves. It is just because he is a priest that no man can afford the mistake of Narcissus. God has not willed us to offer alone; he has called us into an almost endless succession of priesthoods: into histories which themselves become agents of history, into twinings which are themselves elements of a fantastic brocade, and into ministries which move continually outward and homeward into the high Priesthood of the Mystical Body itself.

IX   The Historic Bind

THERE are no doubt many forests through which the complexities of man's oblation of his fellow man may be hunted. To enter them all would be more exhausting than rewarding. Accordingly, I choose to explore only one: the family. At its edges I may touch briefly on friendship, but the family is, I think, a dense enough wood to keep us all busy for at least as long as we have energy and time.

The wood, the forest, the *apeiron*—the place where you are so crowded by detail that you cannot see the horizon, cannot grasp shape, direction, meaning. It makes a good first metaphor for the family. We enter marriage as we enter a wood: with purpose, with hope, with direction. We continue in marriage as we continue in a wood: confused, haunted, and imminently lost. And we survive marriage as we survive a wood: by a combination of dumb luck, faulty knowledge and helpless good will—and at the price of coming through with no thinnest skin left upon a single tooth in our heads. It is a great hike when it is over, but the campfires at which its praises are sung are seldom the ones we light in the forest.

You have read far enough in this book to be, if not convinced of, perhaps used to the idea that the marriage of two persons is a deliberate and priestly attempt to make history. That much has at least a certain clarity, a simple elegance about it that delights the mind. But if anyone expects elegance like that after he has slipped between the sheets of the marriage bed, he should be instructed to pray for patience while he waits. It is a long time coming back. Therefore, if the concept of the priesthood of Adam can strike even a spark in the thick darkness of family life—if the idea of person as the agent of history can explain even *in*elegantly what on earth is going on around our beds and boards—let us by all means see what it has to offer. We have precious little time to lose.

❦

Take John Smith. Add Mary Jones. Mix with a *soupçon* of benefit of clergy, and you have, as already indicated, Smiths. Better than that. You have *the* Smiths: like *the* Bronx, they are an entity arthrous and articulated, a singular and historic city.

Next, take your Smiths and tuck firmly in bed. Set aside for a while to let the initial leaven of their historic choice work. When nearly doubled in bulk, remove, bake and cool under weights. It is a recipe that will make enough history to serve a regiment.

Consider, first of all, the children a marriage brings into being. In the act of conception, through the months of gestation, during the hours of birth, and for a fair number of years after that they are really beings without a history of their own. The child in the womb may be a historic being, but the only history he is involved in is his mother's.

And the child in the cradle, the toddler in the pen, is not much different. The portrait of a young couple with their first baby is still an elegant one. But the snapshot of a pair of beaten forty-five-year-olds surrounded, overshadowed and stymied by a handful of teen-agers and a clutch of elementary school pupils has less to recommend it on the level of intelligibility. Somewhere in between, elegance left by the back door. Around the end of toddling and the beginning of talking, a second and unnoticed pregnancy began; another and quite painless delivery was accomplished. A *person* was born. A piece of history began to distinguish itself and quietly proceeded to start a history of its own. A new priest was ordained *sub rosa* and sent back to his old haunts, with no collar and no letters of ordination, but with all the powers of the priesthood of Adam.

From there on, the story of childhood is the classic story of the unrecognized prince in his rightful kingdom. His poor parents are totally unprepared for his claim. With immense good will, they struggle like peasants and villagers to find out what is going on, but they are always several episodes behind the story. The pains of childhood— the agonies of the teens—are due precisely to the emergence of a priestly agent among beings that are not ready to have him arrive so soon. The common phrase for the process— "cutting the apron strings"—is dull and unenlightening. It provides no reason for the event; it describes it only by means of an external analogy. And, worse yet, it leaves parents with no consolation whatsoever. After all, they provided the best apron strings they knew how to make; and they tied them for the best of all possible reasons: the child's safety and profit; and they know for certain that, at the age of thirteen or fourteen, this fractious string-chopping beast in their midst is still a good six or sixteen years away from being able to manage his own affairs with either safety *or* profit.

But if they would see his rebellion not as a destructive cutting, but as a legitimate (if misunderstood) request by one priest to another to be allowed to say his own Mass—well, that softens the blow a bit. The apparent rejection then becomes a step *toward* history, not away from it. Mind you, I do not think teen-agers see it that way; but I do think that that is what they are up to, even if none of us understands it. They are trying to get clear enough of my priestly grasp so that they can come back at me with a historic grip of their own. They began, you see, with no history but mine; in order for that history to become theirs, it has to be freely lifted up by them. They cannot simply accept my first city with them—from their point of view that was too much like necessity. If our last city is to be built at all, it will not be enough that I invited *them*; they must, somewhere, somehow, invite *me*.

And to do that—to make their invitation recognizable to us both—there must sometime come a refusal of invitation. A tentative rejection preliminary to a voluntary acceptance. It is not a case of doing evil that good may come. What I am talking about is not an evil; it is only a move in the game of oblation. That it is, in a fallen world, commonly accompanied by—even drowned in—attendant evils, argues nothing against the fundamental sanity and reasonableness of the game. And this is only what wise parents have always known and what foolish parents, in rare moments of wisdom, have always suspected: that if you take them lightly, they will love you sooner. Slap them down as a mother cat does her bumptious kittens, but never do less than the cat. Forget it all till the next time; bear them no grudges. We are not making scores here; we are making history. New priests are always obnoxious. Don't stifle the one thing that can save them.

Needless to say, however, such advice is hard to follow. The marvel is that any parents manage to act on it at all. They are thrust, by their parenthood, into a position of almost crippling disadvantage: there is no such thing as cumulative experience in the home. Each of the budding priests in their household begins to offer at his own surprising time and in his own startling way. That my first son does not reject me this year is no guarantee that he will not reject me next—or that my third daughter will not rebel with a vengeance when she turns twelve. We are called to no rehearsals, only public performances. The pieces we so carefully practice are the very ones we will never be asked to play again. Everything that matters has to be read at sight.

To his father and his mother, a newborn baby is only a marvelous *it*: *child* is commonly a neuter word. They know, of course, that he will soon be more than that, but the full weight of their knowledge does not press upon them at first: he becomes a priestly agent only slowly. For a long time he remains more a pet than a person; and through all those lovely years, they practice offering him *as* a pet. But by the time they are able to do it really well, they discover, to their pain and confusion, that such treatment is the one thing in the world which he, in his new-found historicity, cannot possibly put up with. As the curtain rises on the crucial performance, they open their assigned parts as parents of teen-agers and find, to their horror, that the music does not contain a single passage in which their hard-won expertise in scales and arpeggios is needed at all. The entire piece is a long-breathed *adagio*— a problem not in fast passage work, but in artistry, phrasing and articulation. They are no better off than rank beginners. To stumble through it at all is a no small success; and if they should be able to grasp even a hint of the outline of its shape, its meaning, in the one awful first and last reading they are allowed—well, that would be a triumph indeed.

❧

Children, however, are related to more than their parents. Their oblations of other members of their families may be different but they are no less complexly historical. Brothers, sisters, close cousins, stand in an equality. They do not arise out of each other's history; they begin their lives as historyless *its* thrown together in the web of a family. There is between them not the clear, elegant, all-or-nothing distinction that exists between parents and infants; there is only the physical distinction of pups in a litter. To be sure, the farther they are apart in age, the more their relationship will tend to approximate that of parent to child. The boy of fourteen is at least a half-trained priest: his often gracious offering of a five-year-old sister proves it handsomely. But his offering of a big brother of sixteen is harder to interpret. The only thing it seems obviously to prove is original sin.

That is why the priestly work of brothers and sisters is in some ways even more exacting than that of parents. They begin without history, without oblation, but somewhere along the line they must step back far enough from all that surrounds them to behold it and offer it freely. They start their life in the midst of a concelebration to which they were only dragged by the hair of their heads—in a Mass which they know so well that it is practically the last thing in the world they will recognize as a Mass. If they are ever to hold their brethren up in priestly hands, they must, with those same priestly hands, first put their brethren down, off and out, just so that they can then pick them up freely. Their first fellowship with them was an imprisonment about which they had no choice. If there is to be a second fellowship, it must be based not on the serving of a common sentence, but on the acceptance of mutual invitations. Only someone who is really *out* can be invited *in*.

The beehive and the ant heap are cities of a sort, but they are cities which are built by the unavoidable necessity of instinct. The cities of men, on the other hand, can be built only by the free and historic oblations of individual persons. The family is not instinctive; it is priestly. There is a great deal about brothers and sisters that will make them look alike, think alike and laugh alike. But there is nothing about them that will make them a *city* except the exercise of their own priesthood. That is why no one can tell in advance how long it will take for given members of a family to turn the necessity of common origin into the virtue of priestly oblation. The most gracious ones may do it by ten or twelve; the surly and the bitter may not even make a start by seventy. It is so easy to give —and to take—umbrage at the crucial work of separation. The operation is designed, of course, to make a free union possible; but error, ignorance, pride and prejudice lie perpetually at the door. There are often gaps—sometimes unclosable gaps—in the history of a family. Sons and father, brothers and sisters misread the purpose of their drawing away from one another. The letting go which was to be a prelude to taking up again, becomes an outright rejection. The break *for* history becomes a break *in* history, and the *we* that might have formed degenerates, not back into thou and thou—that is an irretrievable condition—but into opposing *hims* or *hers*. The second person singular must rise to the first plural, or sink below itself to the third: *she* is only the cat's mother.

The weaving of the web of a close family, therefore, while it is one of nature's noblest works, is also one of her most difficult. That, I think, is why we generally find that it is our relatives at one remove who, in fact, become our first true consanguine oblations. It is the children of our parents' brothers and sisters with whom we commonly fall into something very like love. "Kissing cousins" is not simply an allusion to dirty games in the attic; it is a hint of the priestliness of man. A boy takes years to get far enough away from his sister even to see what she really looks like, let alone enter into a priestly mutuality with her.

But the same boy may very well accomplish just that in the course of ten minutes with his cousin Mary at the age of twelve. That he will no doubt go on to try to accomplish a good deal more than that—or, better said, less than that, other than that—is beside the point. That is not what makes the oblation, but what unmakes it. He has seen *somebody* with his own eyes; the proclamation of *us* as an offered city, as opposed to *us* as an unavoidable crowd, has gone thundering through the fibres of his being.

But perhaps the chiefest and easiest of the early oblations of children is the lifting up not of their cousins, but of their cousins' parents. It is in the offering of uncles and of aunts that we first use our priestly powers. Long before we can see our parents, we look with gladness upon their brethren. There is no greater historical gift than a brace, a set—a baker's dozen, if at all possible—of uncles. (Dutch uncles will do as well as blood uncles; indeed the inequities of nature make them almost indispensable. No boy's priesthood should be imperiled just because his grandparents failed to have enough children.)

I distrust mightily the modern world's love of sorting people into all kinds of aptitude and ability groups at early ages, but, if I were called upon to do it, I would be interested in only one division; the separation of the unpriestly from the priestly. And I stand ready with a one-question test which will do the job infallibly. *Any ten-year-old boy who would not rather live with his Uncle Henry is a boy to be watched with the gravest suspicion:* his priesthood should have been operative long since. He will not be able to choose his own father for years, but, if he cannot offer his uncles now, we may well have an unhistoric monster on our hands. Such a boy should not, of course, be banished. He needs help, therapy, treatment. Accordingly, he should be provided, perhaps at the government's expense, with a deluxe set of uncles for oblation. A 210-pound water skier, for a start, and a 140-pound model locomotive builder to go with him. And, if available, a poetry reader, a crane operator, an amateur violinist and a judge of good whiskey. And, above all, an uncle who can tell jokes which will grow hairier as the boy grows taller. His cure would not be long coming. The therapy is well-nigh infallible.

Beyond the confines of the family, however, the possibilities for early and instant oblation multiply and abound. One of the saddest features of our present mode of life is the continuing disappearance of the town, the village, the neighborhood. There are neighbors who are even more easily offered than uncles! But if the young are not exposed to them, if there are no stoops and porches to display them, no open basement windows through which to address them, no back fences across which to reach out to them— if there are only barren apartment corridors and porchless development houses—the world has ceased to be the seminary it might have been.

Nonetheless, the priesthood of Adam fights back. Even in the desert of the modern world, children still walk with open, wondering eyes. They offer whatever neighbors they can find, and the offerings they make are often their best as well as their first. The oblations they make later will be more conscious and, therefore, more self-conscious.

Pride grows along with priesthood; the ability to wreck increases with the power to build. But, man and boy, they —and we—offer.

God binds us into histories we did not choose that we may go forth from them into cities of our own shaping. The actual offerings we make in the confines of family and neighborhood are seldom as important as the habit of oblation that we form in the first years of our priesthoood. Give a child only reality and open eyes—give him a father to struggle with and a mother to misunderstand, give him cousins to kiss and aunts to make him pies, give him uncles to offer and large neighbors for oblation—and you will, by every one of those exchanges, move the world another inch away from chaos. It takes more than that to build the city, but without that, it cannot be formed at all.

X   The Black Mass

HILAIRE BELLOC says somewhere that nothing is so hard as ending a book. He advances a number of reasons, chief among them the home truth that there is always something more to be said. I would like, without dissenting from his original motion, to offer an amended and more precise version: there is nothing so hard as making it possible to end a book. The trick of turning a really neat back splice is not accomplished at the end of the rope; you must begin a certain distance in, tie a proper crown knot and work carefully from there. The neatness and elegance of the finished splice depends on preparation.

But more than that, it depends on the proper handling of the reversals of direction in the rope itself. There are very few subjects of any importance which can be ended by proceeding straight ahead. One of the neglected categories in literary criticism is what I would call the Grand Adversative—the *But* Paramount—of a book. It is the point at which the author, having built his case by paying attention to matters of his own choosing, begins to feel the pressure of other matters he has so far kept at bay. He has achieved consistency by selection, but—there it is, you see: *But*—there are all kinds of inconsistencies waiting for him among the things as yet unselected.

If he does not deal with them—if he omits entirely the Grand Adversative—his book will not end at all, but simply unravel like an unspliced rope. If, on the other hand, he tries to tie up his loose ends with assurances from other and alien subjects, his book will end all right, but it will lack the naturalness and integrity it might have had. A rope can indeed be whipped over with string—the problem of mere unravelling can be solved from the outside—but it cannot then be said that the rope itself has a good end. The string has come in as a *deus ex machina* to save the day. Accordingly, if a book is to have both an end and an *honest end*, the author will have to do precisely what a good seaman does: he must use only his proper subject, tie the crown as best he can, and splice backwards. He must take up the But Paramount with both hands and work it right into the heart of the matter.

᪥

Concede the validity of the concept of the priesthood of Adam. Concede further the effectiveness of all the allusive arguments for it based on marsh reeds and marriage beds, on kissing cousins and offered uncles. Concede even, *per impossibile*, that this entire book so far has achieved triumphantly all that it set out to do. Concede all that, and you will still have every right to be sceptical about the whole business. I have showed you some marvelous passages of history; *but*.

But. Your history does not look much like them. But. The world's history does not look much like them. And, for a final, honest But: my own history, my family's history and my parish's history do not look much like them. There is just enough correspondence with them to make the argument temptingly plausible. But on any given day there is more than enough bad history, wrong history, *un*history, to send it sprawling every time. My relations with my children, my parents and my uncles are anything but gorgeous and grand. We all hold innumerable mortgages on each other and we have frequently threatened foreclosure. Oblation has run only a poor second to use. And my relations with my parish and with the many others who have had the questionable fortune to get within shouting distance of me, are not much better. If we are making history here, we are making it in exceedingly small quantities. Adam may be the agent of meaning, but he takes a lot of days off. Most of the time it's hard to believe that anyone is minding the store.

And the same is true of the rest of the world, as you know perfectly well. Most marriages are poor oblations at best: shoddy offerings by lazy priests. And a good many of them are worse than that: demonic oblations, perversions of priesthood, *black Masses*. And if you add only the contents of one issue of a daily newspaper—if you look only at one previous day's record of what man has done about history in politics or in architecture, in love, law or religion—you have come to a perfectly adequate statement of the But Paramount in the subject of the priestliness of man.

Be sure, however, that you state it correctly. It is not the simple adversative involved in the sentence: All right, grant that Adam is the priest of the world; but why, then, doesn't the world look better than it does? That is only a *But* Paravail, an enlargement of the semi-colon. It raises no problem that priestliness cannot explain. The question it asks can be answered, simply and honestly, by saying that the world is a mess because man has been a false and wicked priest. Indeed, I have already said as much long since. The But Paramount, on the other hand, is a deeper and more majestic consideration—one which appears not in the first sketches of the argument, but only in the large and nearly finished drawing. It is the adversative contained in this passage: Grant everything you have said about priesthood and history. Grant also the perversion of priesthood as the explanation of bad history. But if priesthood is the reason for both history and *un*history, must you not despair for good of ever achieving meaning at all?

That But, you see, is no mere elaboration of a semi-colon; it is a word with power, a dark and sovereign lord. Though it speaks in a question, it utters a challenge. For it sees clearly that if it is man the priest who makes history, and man the priest who wrecks history, then history is a subject that may as well be dropped. It looks the author straight in the eye and says: You have produced a tender and amusing account of meaning, *but you can't make it stick*! You have shown us man the priest continually bent upon shaping; you have displayed his love of offerings *in order that* . . . of oblations *for* . . . of priestly acts *so that* . . . . But to all of it, the real story of Adam simply says: So what? So nothing! Sew buttons on your old man's coat! If man builds only to break, if the architect of meaning spends most of his time in the wrecking business, why bother with him at all? *Carpe diem,* or take the gaspipe, but don't waste your time trying to make sense out of nonsense. The wound is incurable; make the patient comfortable and quit.

There, at last, is the real problem of history: not that man neglects it, but that even when he works at it he perverts it. Take a marriage that, after five years or ten, goes bad. Talk to the people involved during the final hours of the shipwreck. There was once, of course, a common history in that marriage: the two of them came together in mutual oblation and jointly shaped a new meaning of their lives. But in those last hours you will be able to find no trace of it. They will have drawn apart into separate histories. As far as they are concerned, the versions they are now presenting are, and always have been, true. But anyone who heard them years before knows better. The long recitals of grievances, the bills of particulars that go into the legal depositions, are precisely *new history*. The old chronicle, the old facts, are indeed still involved; but they have become the elements of a new and sinister offering.

"On the night of April 7th, 1960, I left the house after an argument with my wife. Upon returning, I found she had locked all the doors and windows. When I tried to gain entrance, she called the police, reporting that a prowler was outside her house. Since my wallet and papers were inside the house, the investigating officer refused for at least ten minutes to believe that I was her husband. This was only one of many such humiliations."

Do you want to know what is sinister about that? At the bottom of the affidavit is a signature and a date: John Smith, 10 June, 1965. Notice: April 7th, 1960; June 10th 1965. Five years. Five years of marriage after the dire event. But, according to them, only five years of waiting until they discovered what it meant, until they found how it could be offered, until they finally made history of it. But that is impossible. The very persistence of the marriage from 1960 to 1965 is proof that there was at least another, and possibly a better, offering of that event, a different and happier oblation. The event was, no doubt, irksome enough at the time, but days or weeks later they probably laughed at it and told it to their friends as a joke at their own expense. That is what is sinister about the new oblation in 1965: it is an unsaying of meaning, a *black Mass*, a reversal of reality, a priestly destruction of history.

When you have seen enough such offerings, you acquire two things: a new appreciation of the power of man to give shape and meaning to events, and a deep dread of the meanings he actually brings forth. You come to a despair over the ability of the white Mass to withstand the perverting power of the black—to an increased awe of priesthood and to a profound distrust of priests. You begin to see how easily unmeaning triumphs over meaning. After all, if a marriage survives for ten years—if it survives even for ten months—the amount of solid, right offering involved must be great indeed. Day after day, week after week, mutual oblations are made in sincerity and truth. And day after day, week after week, to some degree at least, even wrong oblations are offered up in forgiveness and love. But once the black Mass begins in earnest, the white one ceases as if it had never been. All the same elements are now present: the same priests, the same altar, the same events. Now however, they are offered backwards and upside down; not for the creation of shape, but for its obliteration. What took years to build is torn down in a month. The whole tissue of mutually offered events in a common life is rent from top to bottom; what survives are two typewritten depositions of five and nine pages respectively.

And if you want to see it writ large instead of small, go from the history of marriage to the history of nations. How much of the priestliness of man has gone into the building of civilization? How many oblations, how many white Masses did it take to build the cities of physics, of music, of poetry? The answer is vast beyond calculation: millions—billions of priests have built and built well. But how much will it take to say the black Mass over it all? Very little. How many matches did it take to burn the library at Alexandria? How many buttons will have to be pushed for the blast that will unsay all the oblations of western civilization?

There, then, is the Grand Adversative in all its power. If fourteen pages of turgid prose can destroy fourteen years of real life, if one affair can wreck a marriage, one betrayal finish a friendship; if one morning's plot can fell a kingdom or one weekend of sedition, privy conspiracy and rebellion put an ancient city in its grave, what chance does meaning really have? The problem of evil is not that there is so much of it that we can't see the good, but that there is so little of it—and yet it still wins.

In the assassination of a Lincoln, a Kennedy, how much was really wrong? Not the gun. The hammer fell with its rightful, authoritative snap, the chamber was its own powerfully rigid self, the powder burned in faithfulness to its nature, and the barrel held the bullet in its course. Was it perhaps the eye of the assassin? No. Light entered the intricacies of its lens, was inverted, fell upon the retina, and was translated infallibly by the brain. Everything was gloriously right; the assassin's aim and the reflex of his finger, the resistance of the wounded flesh and the effectiveness of the bullet itself. A vast concert of things true to themselves, and only one thing really wrong: a priest saying Mass backwards. But that one thing is enough: the flower of a generation slumps in the seat, an era ends, and the tissue of meaning breaks beyond repair.

Cease ye from man, whose breath is in his nostrils: for wherein is he to be accounted of? It is his very priesthood that destroys the world. *This is my first and my last saying, that it had been better not to have given the earth unto Adam: or else, when it was given him, to have restrained him from sinning. O thou Adam, what hast thou done? for though it was thou that sinned, thou art not fallen alone, but we all that come of thee. For what profit is it unto us, if there be promised us an immortal time, whereas we have done the works that bring death? And that we should be shewed a paradise, whose fruit endureth forever, wherein is security and medicine, since we shall not enter into it?*

(For we have walked in unpleasant places.) After all our offerings and sweet savours, after all our tenderness and high good humor, we shall lie low in the grasses. We scatter the ashes of our history in the dust; the city of our solemnities sits broken and solitary. The last shape man imposes upon the world is without form or comeliness; Adam's final word of meaning consists only of the unsaying of the Mass he should have offered.

❧

We come at last, therefore, to the question that has been waiting for us in the heart of history: What can be done with wrong history—with meaninglessness—to keep it from wrecking everything? The answer leads straight into paradox.

First of all, wrong history cannot be offered, must not be offered. It is perversion, reversal, denial; if it is touched at all, if it is admitted for one hour, it corrupts everything. The lie that is admitted into the tissue of a marriage destroys the tissue forthwith. The bigotry that is actually offered up by the priestly hands of a society—that is taken in *as* bigotry, and *as* right—gives that society an incurable wound.

But, secondly, wrong history cries to be offered, must be offered. Man builds the web by taking all things into his priestly hands and lifting them into the exchanges of the city. If even one evil, if even a single piece of wrong history fails to be offered, the city will go down in defeat.

If the power of darkness cannot somehow be taken into the tissue of the web, it will destroy the web as it always has.

Thus the paradox: Evil *must not* be offered, for it corrupts the priest; evil *must* be offered, or else the priest will have no power over it. Let me follow it a little further. We have words for all the possible oblations of wrong history. For the mere rejection of it, we have *blame* and *condemnation*; for the mere acceptance of it, we have *condonation* and *winking at iniquity*; and, for the paradoxical act which accepts and rejects it at once, we have *forgiveness*.

Once again, take a marriage. Into that marriage admit an affair, and into the affair admit eventual disclosure. Behold, you are ready to write a treatise on the oblation of evil. Assume the husband is the—let us avoid words which raise questions—the perpetrator of the affair, the *agent* of it. His wife then becomes the spectator of it, the one against whom, before whom, *to* whom it is done—let us call her the *patient* of the affair.

For the *agent*, the priestly possibilities of the situation are four: he will first attempt to keep the affair from becoming a priestly problem by leading two lives, by offering at two altars. For as long as nobody important finds out, and for as long as he has the stamina and the interest to put up with the wear and tear, he will be able to avoid facing the fact that he is only one priest, and the shaper of only one history. Needless to say, the days of such double offerings are the golden days of an affair, the times of plural benefices and of fat livings in the country. They are the happy times before the reformers move in and spoil everything.

We have, however, already admitted the thing that ends them. The agent's wife finds out, and the fat is in the fire. So far he has avoided the terrible demands of his priesthood: He has not used it to make history, but to play at histories. But now he finds that even his play has been a making. The double life, the double history, turns out to be a painful and unmanageable fact. Enter here, therefore, the really relevant possibilities for his priesthood: blame, condonation, or forgiveness.

Blame. If he simply rejects the history of his affair—if he, in a paroxysm of remorse, blames himself, torments himself, condemns himself—he will hardly escape what he has made. Short of suicide, no man's remorse is proof against passion and involvement. Shame is not a viable ascetical notion; blame is a sleazy theological concept. He will, for a while, stay clear of his mistress; but by and by he will, like Jeshurun, wax fat again and kick, and the last state of that man will be worse than the first.

On the other hand, if he simply accepts what he has done—if he *condones* the affair, glories in it, justifies it— he is no better off. He is, and remains, a being of one history who is trying to function in two. He will learn soon enough that the others in his history—his wife, his mistress—are beings of one history themselves. He may condone the arrangement, but when all is said and done, they probably will not. He will be attempting an offering

which the other sharers in his priesthood—his concele-
brants—will not put up with. Late or soon, he will find
himself with one altar only—and badly shaken in the
bargain.

Let me set aside for a moment the *forgiveness* which
the agent must extend to himself, and turn to blame or
condonation as they are found in the *patient*—in his wife.

Should she attempt merely to reject, to blame her husband, she destroys the very offering in whose name she
issues the rejection. To be sure, she cannot, any more
than he, *accept* the affair; but if she simply blames, she
rejects her husband along with it. He may have been a fool
to divide his history, to inaugurate two concelebrations,
but, fool or not, he has done it, and in dead earnest. The
more profound her rejection, the more scathing her blame
toward him, the more effectively she destroys the only real
Mass she herself has to say.

But if she condones, she does no better, for then she
becomes another foolish priest, another ineffectual architect of two meanings, two histories, where only one is
possible. Blame may be destructive, but at least it recognizes
the realities of the situation. Condonation is monstrous.
The "understanding" foursome who have swapped wives
and husbands are engaged in a collegial black Mass for the
unsaying of all their meanings. The "intelligent" couple
who wink at each other's iniquity and arrange a white-
washed marriage, or a cool and passionless divorce, wreck
history in the name of happiness. And, without going into
it, the society which makes it increasingly possible for such

impossibilities to be achieved is a society which is sick at the heart. It is trying to preserve the city without preserving the priestliness which alone can build it.

It is *forgiveness*, then, which, in both agent and patient, is the only viable priestly exercise. Forgiveness in the *agent* as the acceptance of priestly responsibility for the impossible history he has made. Forgiveness *toward himself* which, without blame and without condonation, accepts the affair, but accepts it *as wrong*. Forgiveness as the only real option in the whole tissue of his life. But forgiveness —mark it well—as an act of almost unimaginable difficulty: forgiveness as a passion, a crucifixion—as an imminent destruction of him by the admission into his being of the awful contradictions he has wrought.

And forgiveness in the *patient* as the same thing: the acceptance of the affair, but the acceptance of it as wrong. A sufferance more gracious than any condonation, and a reproof more austere than any blame. A more awful forgiveness, no doubt, for no agent sees his monstrousness as it is in the eyes of his victims. And a deeper passion, a more deadly cross, a more certain destruction, for no agent feels the full force of what he has done to his patient. But without the acceptance of suffering there can be no forgiveness. History is made, or unmade, by the *acts* of Adam the priest; but history can be saved only by his *passion*. Unless evil is taken *out*, the city cannot be built; but unless it can be taken *up*, it cannot be taken out at all. Somehow therefore, man must rise above both blame and condonation—they leave only wrong history free to roam at large—and he must enter into the high mystery by which it is—not destroyed—but offered, hidden, *sequestered*, in the heart of the passion of the priest.

ॐ

I do not intend to belabor the point much beyond that. The last reversal of the Grand Adversative is already in sight. It is simply this: But who can afford to be that kind of priest? For the lighter and lesser perversions of history we may all do well enough. The sins of ignorance, the catastrophes which, almost accidentally, grew greater than anyone meant them to be, the evils which, even by the victims, were never felt in all their dark power—these we can manage. Inattention spares us the full assessment of the cost. But with the recognition of *deliberate* evil by the agent, and with the bearing of the *full weight* of it by the patient—there, the oblation begins to be expensive.

It is not enough to say it demands charity. That is hardly a candid answer. Anyone who finally sees what is involved will realize that such charity is not only rare; it is deadly. Evil is no mere diagram; it is the power of darkness, and it can do things—vast and ugly things— to anyone who, even to forgive it, gets close to it. To offer up evil in a passion of forgiveness is, for all practical purposes, to let evil have its way, and, in all likelihood, to be destroyed by it. The passion is followed by a crucifixion, and the crucifixion by death and the tomb.

And pacifism is not the answer either. It is still another

instance of an error that is only an inch away from the truth. As a diagram of the passion, as an insistence that the only way to get evil *out* is to take it *in*, it is right. But as it is commonly presented, that is, as a recipe for the effective conquest of evil—as a formula to end wars—it is impossible. The only logical result of pacifism is the death of the pacifist. Evil is much too ambitious to be impressed by the idea that easy targets should not be hit.

If, therefore, there is ever to be a Passion that will turn the trick, if there is to be an Agent with hands clean enough not to be defiled by the poison of his own guilt, if there is to be a Patient with a heart great enough to face the monstrousness of evil and still be willing to take it in— if there is to be a Pacifist who can survive his own charity —something will have to be done to the priesthood of Adam. It will need not only *repair* to restore it to its natural operation, but also *enlargement* to raise it to a new and mysterious working, by which it can be defeated and still win. What then?

Two things. First of all, human nature must not be discarded. Man is the priest of the world; to build the city without him, to make history run its course apart from his ministrations, would be victory at the price of junking the world we know. The new priest, therefore, must be man. But secondly, for the renovation, human nature alone is not enough. Somehow, the second Adam will have to be able not only to survive, but to triumph gloriously over the disaster of his charity. And for that—I shall, as I promised, say it out at last—you need God. Not a *deus ex machina* who comes in to save the day by irrelevant marvels, but a *Deus Incarnatus* who can be man enough to die in his priesthood, but God enough to rise from the dead.

I said I would not belabor the point. I shall not. By the grace of God we have such a redeemer: Jesus Christ, the Incarnate Word, the Second Adam, the Great High Priest. He was despised and rejected. He walked among us and the world said a black Mass over him. But in his Death and Passion, in his Resurrection and Ascension, he takes all our words and reads them right again. Ever since, with or without conviction, we have made that offering the determining point of history: the Cross is where the triumph of meaning becomes possible. Without the victory of evil that it permitted, so much history would have been lost that salvation would be meaningless. But without the sequestering of evil that it achieved—without the taking of meaninglessness into the heart of the only Priest who could afford it—the City would forever go unbuilt.

He has tied, you see, a back splice to end all back splices. In the very nick of time—at the end of history's rope—the tongues of flame in-fold into the crowned knot of fire, and the fire and the rose are one.

XI Epilogue

LECTOR: Well?

AUCTOR: Well, what?

LECTOR: That sounded like an end to me. Do I assume correctly that that is all you have to say?

AUCTOR: Yes and no. Belloc was right. An author can go on more or less indefinitely; but it is best if his book does not.

LECTOR: What do you feel you have omitted?

AUCTOR: Aha! You will not catch me as easily as that. I have made whatever argument I can manage for my case. The rope is spliced back. If it does not reach you, I am sorry; you must cast about for a longer piece.

LECTOR: You have nothing to add then?

AUCTOR: I did not say that. If you like, I can end as I began: *next to*, but not *on*, the subject.

LECTOR: But is that consistent with your principles?

AUCTOR: Consistency is the hobgoblin of small . . .

LECTOR: Never mind. Just end.

AUCTOR: I must ask you then to join me in a recurrent— not fantasy, but—distracted occupation of mine.

LECTOR: I am in your hands.

AUCTOR: Today is Friday. In the Latin, that is *feria sexta,* the sixth day of the week. On the sixth day, according to the first chapter of Genesis, God made the living creatures of the earth: cattle, creeping thing and beast. A little later in the same day he also made man in his image and after his likeness: male and female; for dominion, for fruitfulness, for multiplication, and for the replenishment of the earth.

LECTOR: Now, really, does anyone in this day and age seriously believe . . .

AUCTOR: I have no idea. I am not addressing myself to the point. Let me finish.

A good while after that, on the Friday of the Preparation of the Sabbath of the Passover, God *remade* man by a passion, a death and a resurrection in the human nature he had taken to himself. As a result, for most of the Fridays since, Christians have undertaken to fast in honor of the day.

LECTOR: May I ask where all this leads?

AUCTOR: There is no need. I am almost there.

Finally, it is a practice among certain Christians to make the day more notable still by the recitation of the English Litany. It is, no doubt, a custom honored more . . .

LECTOR: Spare me that. I gather I am about to be invited to pray.

AUCTOR: Yes and no again. I began by taking you on a walk. I end likewise. The Litany is a devotion designed to be used *in procession*, a prayerful circumambulation, if you will, of the City. The church walks through the world, and in her passing she lifts all things into her oblation: marsh reed and shabby village, offered uncle and broken marriage. No triumph of priesthood is too high for her attention; no failure, no distraction irrelevant to the Passion by which she returns history to God. Even if you do not pray, come these last few steps, just for the walk.

༂

O God the Father, Creator of heaven and earth;
Have mercy upon us.
O God the Son, Redeemer of the world;
Have mercy upon us.
O God the Holy Ghost, Sanctifier of the faithful;
Have mercy upon us.
O holy, blessed, and glorious Trinity, one God;
Have mercy upon us.

The day before yesterday, I drove through a suburban development. I saw there:

three women gossiping at the end of a driveway;

five pre-school children playing with toy dumptrucks;

a man, obviously a husband, repositioning a lawn sprinkler in accordance with his wife's shouted **directions**;

  a man, obviously a salesman, leaving his parked
car and knocking on the door of a house;

  another man, not obviously either a husband
or a salesman, walking in a front door without
knocking;

  three women still gossiping, but more ani-
matedly than before.

Why, O Lord, do we do it? What was it that we had in
mind? Why are we so bent on toys and lawns, on marriages
and assignations? Pity us, Lord; this is all the city we
have. We mean well, O God; we mean to *mean*. We have
done nothing here that was not the fruit of our priesthood.
Why do we not build better? Why do our children hate
us, why must our neighbors talk, why are our husbands
so closed?

Remember not, Lord, our offences, nor the offences
of our forefathers; neither take thou vengeance of our
sins; spare us, good Lord, spare thy people, whom thou
hast redeemed with thy most precious blood, and be not
angry with us forever.

Spare us, good Lord.

  Wednesday night, first jointly, then in separate interviews, a married couple told me;

  that they had both retained lawyers;

  that they both had their faults, but that it was
no sense trying again if the other party wouldn't
try too;

  that his wife was sick;

that her husband was sick;
that he hit her;
that he never really hit her;
that his mother ran his life;
that her mother ran her life;
that the church was unreasonable to expect
people to go on forgiving.

O Lord, what did we do wrong? All we wanted was to build; why do we live now in ruins? Spare us the misery of our priesthood.

From all evil and mischief; from sin; from the crafts and assaults of the devil; from thy wrath; and from everlasting damnation,

Good Lord, deliver us.

On Thursday morning, I went, as usual, for my walk, and bought, as usual, my daily copy of *The New York Times*:

HUMPHREY THINKS WAGNER WILL RUN
Senate Bars Ending Aid to U.N. Debtors

O Word Incarnate, we are in love with meaning; we are obsessed with 44-point caps and with 30-point upper and lower case. We impose shape endlessly; but history escapes us still. O Wisdom, who reachest from one end to the other, and mightily and sweetly orderest all things: Come and build the city for us in thy Passion.

From all sedition, privy conspiracy and rebellion; from all false doctrine, heresy, and schism; from hardness of heart, and contempt of thy word and commandment,
    Good Lord, deliver us.

On Thursday afternoon, I said prayers for a man in the last extremity of life. A sad trickle of saliva lay in the corner of his mouth. Uphold him, O God, in the communion of the Catholic Church, and in the confidence of a reasonable, religious, and holy hope; and uphold us all, O Lord, in the face of a meaningless end to seventy-three years of meaning.

I walked home and smelled liver and onions on a side street. A man would be a fool not to come home to such a wife. Drive despair from us, O most Merciful.

By thine Agony and Bloody Sweat; by thy Cross and Passion; by the precious Death and Burial; by thy glorious Resurrection and Ascension; and by the Coming of the Holy Ghost,
    Good Lord, deliver us.

This morning, I rehearsed with my sons: three pieces from the *Musica Brittanica*. The Lupo *Pavan* went best: the ornamentation began to come out right. But one of them yawned while he was playing, and the other breathed in the wrong place. I became angry and abusive.

Tonight I play a concerto for recorder and chamber orchestra. It is all over now but the post mortems. "Don't think about getting through it; think only of playing musically. The Siciliano must lilt; the downbeats must lift, not fall. The entrance after the second *tutti* in the *allegro assai* must be proclaimed with brilliant articulation."

Accept in mercy, O Lord, whatever it is that we so weakly have in mind. Spare, O God, in the universal shipwreck of the world, our love of shape and meaning, and grant that we have not trained these hands only to unstring them in death. In spite of fears, make us bold in our priesthood. Lift for us, O Lord. Lift our places and our times, lift creek and harbor, Tom and marsh reed, lift even broadloom and vinyl; receive into thy Passion all that we build, and in thy ruin make us whole again.

In all time of our tribulation; in all time of our prosperity; in the hour of death and in the day of judgement,

Good Lord, deliver us.

ℰ

I leave you there. The walk is as wide as the City; the Litany is as large as life itself, and no distraction is alien to it. Caught up in the Passion, we plead freely for the laborers in the vineyard and for the unity of nations, for the restoration of the erring and for the comfort of the weak-hearted; and for women in childbirth, for prisoners and captives, for the fatherless children and widows—for all men everywhere who, in the priesthood of Adam, have said their Masses and laid away their vestments, who have offered as they could afford, but who found history too expensive for them; who, if they are to build the City at all, will build it only in the Passion of a better Priest than Adam.

For, by the disaster of his charity, God plays out at last the Game that began with the dawn of history. In the Garden of Eden—in the paradise of pleasure where God laid out his court and first served the hint of meaning to man —Adam strove with God over the tree of the knowledge of good and evil. But God does not accept thrown-down racquets. He refuses, at any cost, to take seriously man's declination of the game; if Adam will not have God's rules, God will play by Adam's. In another and darker garden he accepts the tree of man's choosing, and with nails through his hands and feet he volleys back meaning for unmeaning. As the darkness descends, at the last foul drive of a desperate day, he turns to the thief on the right and brings off the dazzling backhand return that fetches history home in triumph: Today shalt thou be with me in *Paradise*.

God has *Gardens* to give away! He has cities to spare! He has history he hasn't even used! The last of all the mercies is that God is *lighter* than man, that in the heart of the Passion lies the divine Mirth, and that even in the cities of our exile he still calls to Adam only to catch the glory, to offer the world, and to return the service that shapes the city of God.

Preface

IF you object that this is an odd place for a preface, my only answer is that this has been an odd book, and that there is no point in trying to switch off the oddity this late in the day. Prefaces are a strange genre anyway. An author may pretend that he is simply addressing a foreword to his readers, but, in fact, he is in the sly business of taking out insurance against reviews that miss the point.

Any policy he buys, however, is of dubious value. For one thing, if a book doesn't make its own point, no preface in the world can save it. For another, if a critic has a tin ear, whistling the same tune in another key won't help. And, for a last, the author's claim on the reader's attention extends only to what he has written, not to what he thinks about it all. Authors are almost the last people in the world who should be allowed to comment on their own books.

That being the case, it would, no doubt, be wisest to suppress the preface altogether. I am torn, however: the cool waters of wisdom only partly quench the thirst for insurance. Accordingly, I give you a preface, but I print it at the end. Here at least, if you read it, you read it when I wrote it—after the book, and after you have come to your own conclusions. And if perhaps you are wise enough

not to read it at all, we part company while we are still
such friends as we have become.

ℰ

Admittedly, this book has been more allusive than direct.
Permit me a brief apologia for the style. The offhanded-
ness is deliberate. I have a conviction that, in the present
shipwreck of philosophy—particularly in the absence of
any working concept of the analogical nature of all dis-
course about God, it is safer not even to attempt to speak
directly. The best of the classical theologians, of course,
had a firm grip on the doctrine of analogy and sprinkled
their works liberally with *caveats* and cries of *nescimus*.
Every theologian worth his salt walked with one foot on
his affirmations and the other firmly planted on the *via
negativa*. Unfortunately, however, a good many of their
heirs, assigns and devisees fell into the trap of thinking that
the categories of traditional dogmatics had somehow succeeded in getting straight at what God and His action were
really like. The result was that the all-important sense of
mystery promptly left by the back door and, with it, the
possibility of germane theology.

After that, the only solution anyone could think of was
to leave the front door open in the hope that germaneness
would wander in off the street. Theology, however, cannot
be saved by inviting other disciplines in to do its work.
We have had sociological theologians and psychological
theologians; we have had mathematical theologians and
evolutionary theologians; and lately we have been treated

to the theologians of linguistic analysis and historical scepticism. None of them has done much to rescue the party from boredom: the gala theological blowout of the age to come turns out to be just one more slow leak.

Germaneness cannot be restored from the outside. The bright new theologians of systematic doubt are no improvement over the bad old theologians of straight-line certainty. The whole lot of them are guilty of trying to deal directly with what can only be handled analogically; the difference between them is simply that in the new breed the failure of analogy has led them to stop talking about God altogether, while the old boys continue to act as if they know more than they do. But silence is no solution. Man goes on talking about God anyway, whether the theologians do or not; he even, on occasion, talks *to* Him. Given that fact, the only responsible thing for theology to do is to try to save its own party by its own methods: that is, it must either formally refurbish the doctrine of analogy, or else it must find a way of speaking that will, informally, do the same thing. In choosing the allusive rather than the direct approach, I have, hopefully, opted for the latter.

I have avoided straight exposition because I think that in a world that has lost the sense of mystery it can only mislead. We do not need to have either God or creation *explained* to us; we are already sick to death of explanations. We have forgotten, you see, not what reality *means*, but how it smells, and what it tastes like. The work of theology in our day is not so much interpretation as contemplation: God and the world need to be held up for *oohs* and *ahhs* before they can safely be analyzed. Theology begins with admiration, not problems. If a man walks through the world doing psychedelic puzzles rather than looking at reality, if he insists on tasting the wine of being with his nose full of interpretive cigarette smoke, the cure is not to hand him better puzzle books or more lectures on wine. He must be invited to *look* at what is in front of him and to get rid of those nasty cigarettes. And that perhaps is the place where this apologia can come to rest as far as the style of the book is concerned: I have written you a little tirade against smoking while you taste how gracious the Lord is.

Having justified my indirection, however, I want to go a little further and try to locate myself in the present theological landscape. Some of the things that I have dealt with allusively can be treated at least a little more directly, and I propose to have a go at three of them. They are: the alienation of man from reality; the nature of God's action in the world; and the place of the Passion of Christ in history. Accordingly, I give you three short essays and, for the present at least, thereafter hold my peace.

ဇ

ALIENATION

We have been treated lately to a number of solemn harpings on the subject of man's estrangement from the world he inhabits. Books and articles conjure up visions of poor old Adam stumbling lost and lone through the automated and computerized age to come. If we are to believe the accounts, humanity is on the verge of technological unemployment. We may feel lonely now, but just wait until the electronic brains do *all* the work.

The menace is generally billed as brand new, but it has a familiar ring to it. It seems to me to be only the latest phase of one of the oldest diseases of modern man: his deep-rooted unwillingness to allow being to be itself, his penchant for over-interpreting the obvious, his refusal to drink his reality neat. Almost from the first moment of his philosophical maturity he is trained to think of the world in terms of a glibly popularized science. "That table over there," the high-school sophomore is told, "is actually not a table at all. It is really a cloud of electrons." For fourteen years Johnny has thought otherwise, but he has been in the dark. Now he is invited—more, he is *told*, on pain of intellectual disgrace—to face the light of the new day.

Obedient boy that he is, Johnny obliges. As he thinks the matter through, he comes to see that his tomato sandwich cannot possibly be a tomato sandwich, and that his breakfast egg is not really an egg. What matters most about everything, he learns, is not what he knows it to be, but some mysterious and abstract stuff that he is told it is made of. Consequently he acquires, at least by implication, a guilty conscience if he decides to spend much time acquiring a taste for such accidental superficialities as *things* and *substances*. If he cares seriously about how his eggs are cooked, he had better not mention it in intellectual circles.

What Johnny finds out eventually, of course, is that

he has been slipped a very tiresome kind of mickey. He is the recipient of a *Weltanschauung* that is a crashing bore. It takes all the fascinatingly solid differences between things and writes them off as only apparent—as merely accidental determinations of an endless and monotonous raw material: the true substance of the world is the tasteless sub-atomic tapioca out of which it is made. And *that* is all he is to be served, not simply for dessert, but for breakfast, lunch and dinner, world without end.

The really fearful thing about such a view is that it stands the world on its head. Real *things*—substantial beings—are written off as of secondary importance: the distinction between sharp razors and dull razors is dismissed as so fine that it hardly matters. The difference between a cooked and an overcooked soufflé is practically nil. It is the infra-nuclear oatmeal that really counts. And, yet, every man in his right mind knows better than that. A dull razor is no razor at all, and is to be cursed roundly. And a dry soufflé . . . well, that is more than sufficient cause for weeping. If you rob man of his right to such rages and tears, you court disaster.

For insofar as he believes what he has been taught, he will become bored, estranged and . . . alienated. The world around him will seem far too accidental for real care. It will be worthy only of manipulation—or worse. And he himself will sit solitarily important in a world which, as he meets it, doesn't *matter*. To be sure, because of the legacy of Christian civilization, he will probably go on believing that somehow man, with his rights and duties, his privileges and obligations—with his individual status as a *person*—does matter. But, on that basis, man is only the last raisin in an ocean of rice pudding. It makes for a lonely life.

Modern man's alienation stems, not from the incidental advances of his technology, but from a philosophy which has turned him into a metaphysical freak: he is the last, inexplicably substantial being in an otherwise relative world. No *thing* keeps him real company. Far from being a materialistic age, we are a devilishly spiritual one. Having forsaken the true concrete individuality of *things*—having made care about differences philosophically disreputable —we are left only with diagrams of reality to keep us going.

At this writing, I learn that my eggs no longer need to be done at all—either to a turn or to a crisp. My super-market will sell me an envelope of powder which, when dissolved, will provide an instant breakfast. No matter that I once thrilled to a nicely boiled egg in a thin china cup. It is time now for me to face the facts of life. Eggs don't matter, and my sensibilities don't rate. All the foolish substantialities of the past must give way to the new truth: what counts is the juxtaposing of my nutribility and the envelope's nutritiveness. And what a confrontation *that* is: abstract cheek laid against immaterial jowl, and the devil take the whole shooting match.

No wonder we're bored. However important the sub-strate of the world may be to scientific analysis, it will not do as a substitute for philosophy. The physical question of what beings are made out of can never be allowed to preempt man's proper metaphysical concern with what being *is*. Man's alienation, his boredom, his estrangement can be cured only by the recovery of a philosophical sanity which will allow him to meet *things* face to face. An egg is an egg, and must be saluted as such. And china is china, and all things are themselves: mushrooms and artichokes, wine and cheese, earth and stars and sky and ocean. It is *things* that matter, and our cure waits for the restoration of our ability to care about them.

It will be an uphill fight, though. Pleasant as the idea sounds, the world is anything but ready for a revival of Christian materialism. It is more than ready for a revival of *religion*, of course, but religion and Christianity are by no means the same thing. The proclamation of the Gospel is the announcement of an embarrassingly concrete and material piece of work by God in history. The salvation it offers operates by the assumption of humanity into the Person of God the Son and by the incorporation of the rest of the race into the sacred humanity so assumed. It is a bit too crass and earthy to rate as a gorgeous piece of spiritual philosophy.

Accordingly, the world's inveterate lust for lovely spiritualities will cause it to look almost anywhere before it seriously considers Christianity and all it implies. The winds of the times have begun to blow out of the East politically and psychologically; if I may venture a little prophecy, I think that they will also shortly blow us a revival of religion. It may well be that the next major intellectual fad will be Oriental spirituality. There are, in fact, signs that it has already begun: the psychedelic cults, with their little trips into the inner spaces of the mind, are the outriders of a movement which will systematically prefer the exploration of "consciousness" to the savoring of *being*. When it arrives in force, religion eastern-style will be the order of the day, and the Judaeo-Christian tradition will have a hard time finding houseroom anywhere except in the basement of unspiritual superstitions.

There will, of course, be attempts to offer spiritualized and, therefore, fashionable versions of Christianity. (The God is Dead movement is, in many respects, a reaction to just that sort of thing. Unfortunately, however, it falls prey to the very errors it opposes. To replace intemperate reliance on the sacred with excessive faith in the secular is to achieve nothing. It simply forces the secular to do the work previously done by the sacred and, by just so much, to lose its true secularity. Christian materialism sees the two orders as complementary, interpenetrating and inseparable, but it never tries to make one of them do the work of the other.) But the greatest damage from the windstorm of the East will not be sustained by Christianity —that can, in time, take care of itself; the real wreckage will be the collapse of any workable notion of history.

If you adopt a philosophical outlook which makes *things* unimportant, you automatically make history meaningless. It is the cats and the alligators, the rivers and the hills, the kings, the bankers and the boys in the back room that make the world the way it is. If you seriously eliminate them from consideration, the only thing left is to import an assortment of gods, fates and ghosts to run the show in their absence. You may manage to make it sound a little like the Gospel, but it will be the furthest thing in the world from it. Christians believe, of course, that God Himself is the ultimate Lord of history, but the Gospel of the Incarnation insists that He does not rule at the price of turning things and men into ciphers. And that brings me to the second little essay.

ႜ

THE ACTION OF GOD IN THE WORLD

The recent debates over the Death of God have managed to propose all the right questions about God and history in almost all the wrong ways. The press, of course, has given the impression that the real point of the discussion was whether God existed or not, and, no doubt, at least a few of the principals in the debate have been guilty of saying as much. At least some of them, however, have seen that the real relevance of their comments lies elsewhere.

Outside the realm of straight dogmatic theology (where the reality of God has always been a *datum* and not a problem), questions about the existence of God must be dealt with in terms of the only subject which has an honest claim on them: metaphysics. Accordingly, the problem of the existence or non-existence of God can hardly be advertised as the hottest issue of the twentieth century, brought to light only recently by new and daring thinkers. Rather, it is a piece of unfinished metaphysical business dating from the eighteenth century in its present form, and from the fourteenth century if you trace it to its roots. It is not the doctrine of God that is the main problem of contemporary theology; it is the doctrine of Man, the doctrine of the Secular, the doctrine of History.

There, you see, is the sad part of the promotion given to the recent debate. Nearly every man Jack of the new theologians has had a lot to say about Secularity, about Culture, about Man, about History. But far too many of them have been shunted off, either by the press or by their own inadequate metaphysic, into a discussion of Deity. Their common sense and good judgment—their feeling for the heart of the matter—landed them squarely in the right neighborhood; but their less than adequate friends talked them into working the wrong side of the street.

Even when they managed to stay on the right side, however, their insistence on a divorce between the sacred and the secular made it difficult for them to arrive at a respectable doctrine of secularity. Modern man's problem, you see, is no more about the nature of the secular, pure and simple, than it is about the nature of God, pure and simple. It is, when all is said and done, about the nature of their interaction. Our confusion is over a world which *simply* does not seem to need God, and over a God who *simply* does not seem to be at work in the world. With our penchant for simplicities, you see, we have managed so to limit both the sacred and the secular that we have set them at odds with each other. I suggest that the only way to get them back together is to get that word *simply* out of the discussion, and to restore to its rightful place the biblical dimension of *mystery*. The world will never be clear to us until we stop insisting that it be plain.

To begin with, the world has never *simply* needed God.

He is too skillful a creator to have left evidence of his direct action lying all over the lot—and He is too serious about creating a world that will stand on its own feet and blow its own nose. Good theologians have always held that God's *immediate* work in creation (that is, the work in which, if you could examine it, you would find God's own hand on the throttle) has always been *mysterious*. God intimately and immediately bestows the act of being upon each existing thing, but that bestowal occurs at the roots of reality. The only evidences of His creativity that you and I can manage to investigate lie higher and are in the realm of His mediate action. Everything that is empirically ascertainable about the world lies in the realm of secondary causes—in the province of gloriously independent *things* which, thank you very much, *simply* act for themselves, but which God, by the *mystery* of His creative act, causes to be. The secular, you see, can be just as secular as it pleases, and never suffer a moment's divorce from the sacred. God constantly holds the world in being, and He constantly pronounces it very good. It is only when the world tries to take its simplicities without a good stiff shot of mystery that it becomes the bore it so frequently is.

That leads to the second point. In this marvelously produced world of secondary causes, God has never (or at least, barring miracle, almost never) acted *simply*. From time to time, He has filled a water pot with wine or provided fish sandwiches for a crowd, but most of the time His action has been more mysterious than that. His relationship to my cleaning of my fingernails, or to your writing of a letter to the editor, or to any of our alliances in love, marriage or politics has been complex. He has caused *us*, without causing *them*; He has been Pure Act without infringing on creation's action; and He has been the sovereign Lord of History who, having bestowed upon each thing its little plot of being, has been content to put up with some fearful and wonderful farming. The courteous Creator of the worlds, if He rules at all, does not seem to rule by simplicities or to guide history along straight lines. His creatures stand *extra nihil* and *extra causas* only by His largesse; but by that same largesse He allows them to act as if they owed nothing to anybody.

His work in the world, therefore, and the world's need of Him, have always been mysterious, inscrutable, anything but self-evident. The presence of the sacred in the secular has been a bit difficult to keep a finger on, and men have accordingly been entirely too ready to abandon the embracing of the mystery in favor of simple sacredness or simple secularism. We have been treated to all kinds of theories about the world, and I have dealt with a number of them in the third chapter. Through it all, however, both the Sacred and the Secular have gone on being their own marvelously and mysteriously interpenetrating selves. No doubt, we should have caught that hint long ago if we had been listening to Scripture or even to such a lowly discipline as dogmatic theology. The classical descriptions of His work in creation, for example, are anything but simplicities. To say that He creates *ex nihilo* is hardly to limit Him to a straight-line approach to the world. And to refer to Him as Necessary Being, or as the *movens non motum*, is to invoke not plain reasons, but logical absurdity as the root of explanation. The note of mystery, of paradox, is the hallmark of classical theology.

And if mystery is the rule in the work of creation, how much more so in redemption? What is the call of Abraham but the announcement of God's action by mysteries rather than by simplicities? He will bless the world in the seed of a man who has no seed, and whose seed He will later command to be destroyed. What is the history of Israel but the story of the peregrinations of the body of the mystery? It is no straight-line success story. Israel's *simple* triumph appears to have occupied a period of about an hour and twenty minutes in the whole history of the world. For the rest, all the way up to its flowering in the Cross, the Resurrection, and the Church, it is a rhapsody of unsuccess, an epic presentation of the theme of God's triumph through failure, of His reasoning through paradoxes, of His action through passion—in a word, of *mystery* as His chosen vehicle.

There, then, is the hint of the true relationship between the sacred and the secular. It has never been a case of simple action or of simple need. To be sure, the world of secondary causes moves in simplicities, small and great. The cat jumps at the mouse, and the iron leaps to the magnet, and men build houses, and nations create institutions—all on intelligible lines. But those very lines are drawn on the utterly mysterious slate of an unnecessary world held in being by Necessity Himself. Again, man tells lies, and he waters stock, and marriages are broken and six million Jews die in ovens—all in nice straight, intelligible lines. But those lines, too, are drawn on the slate of the secular held in being by the sacred. And in their case (which is the case of the world as it is now) it is precisely the Passion of Christ through which the sacred mysteriously rules history. And that brings me to the last essay.

ಌ

HISTORY AND THE PASSION

In chapters ten and eleven, I spent some time on the point that without the Passion of Christ, and without an unceasing intention to draw all that we are and have into that Passion, no history can be saved. I held the point off until the end of the book, and even then hit it only one more or less direct blow. It was part of the allusive approach. Nevertheless, though the blow was lightly struck, the point about the Passion is, in fact, the point of the book, and I want to enlarge a little upon it here.

That the world does not accept Christ Crucified comes as no surprise. The Cross is not pretty. Worse yet, it is paradoxical, scandalous, vulgar and, all in all, far beneath the dignity of anyone the world is willing to recognize as God. It is, as St. Paul said a long time ago, a stumbling block to the Jews and a lot of foolishness to the Greeks. What does come as a surprise, though, is the fact that the Church seems to find it as hard to swallow as the world. The one group of people who should be expected to find it the wisdom and power of God in history are the very ones who, more often than not, try to unload it at the earliest possible moment. We preach almost anything before we preach Christ Crucified. The upshot of it is that the world finds both our diagnoses and our prescriptions irrelevant.

We have talked so often about soundness and sanity that we have given ourselves and our age the impression that the goal of Christianity is the miraculous achievement of health and goodness here and now—that history is to be repaired simply, and from the outside. Worse yet, we have tacitly suggested that Christianity will be manifested best and chiefly by the healthy and the good, which usually ends up meaning (God help us) by us. The church has more or less openly hoped that it could be a kind of free ulcer-clinic, AA chapter and general faith-healing dispensary—the very present help that could keep man out of the clutches of the head shrinkers and medicine men.

This was, perhaps, inevitable. After all, we do believe in a God who restores all things—we do confess the triumph of goodness. We say to the sick world; Come here and be cured: be healed of your ills, be made whole of your maladjustments, be lifted up in triumph over your vices. God wills your health, your balance, your goodness; come, take Grace, and rise.

It is all true. But we have acted as if it were the whole truth or, better said, as if we could safely state it that way to fallen man and have him get it right. As a matter of fact, however, something more must always be added. Tell him that much, illustrate it with Jesus' miracles of healing, root it in the general beneficence of God, and he will inevitably draw himself a Mary Baker Eddyish picture of

Christianity which will not square either with the Gospel or with life.

Take Christ's miraculous acts of healing. How universal were they? How far should they be allowed to form the basis for our everyday expectations? How many of all the sick did He cure? How many demoniacs did He heal? Not many by any estimate—far too few to touch the aggregate misery even of His own day. His cures themselves were always more like signs than solutions. Lazarus went to a second grave: he was raised from the dead, but not from dying. His real problem was met elsewhere than in the miracle. And the rest of the Gospel picture is the same. Those whom Christ cured by His miracles remained fundamentally what they were—creatures still trapped in the agony of a fallen world. Either He must have a deeper remedy or He was guilty of merely symptomatic treatment, of giving anodynes to the incurable. Unless He has succeeded on another level, His program of healing here and now is not only a failure, but a cruel one.

The same point can be proved by the pastoral ministry, if we are honest enough to take a good look at it. How often are the disturbed really calmed? How many marriages headed for the rocks actually manage to avoid them? How many destructive loves do we ever succeed in taming? Not many. We kid ourselves into thinking we are successful healers by the expedient of writing off the vast army of incurables. But they are not cured for all that. By and large, the unhealed simply leave our studies and our pews and take their sickness somewhere else. The loudest and clearest offer they heard from us was the outside chance of a miracle here and now, and, when that failed us, we failed them. How must our Gospel of simple healing have sounded? What must it be like to hear only a medicinal or a psychiatric Christ? Must they not gather that we have a message only for a select clientele—that we are all right for the resilient and for the well-endowed by luck and nature, but that we will not do for the common run of humanity who know that they are trapped in their agony and are not about to bounce back? Mustn't our message to them sound like the harsh and uncomplimentary word of Christian science to the incurable: Sorry, Charlie, but the trouble is yourself; you need to work up some more faith before you can play in our league. Monstrous!

Of course, the whole trouble is themselves. They knew that; that is why they came. But that we should make it sound as if their problem is after all a matter of a human more or less, that we should hint ever so subtly that with us the trouble has ceased to be ourselves, that the passion is over and that, in us who have the first fruits of the spirit, the creature no longer groans and travails—this is what confounds them. God forgive us. To them, it must be as if the Gospel had never been preached; as if Christianity were only a miraculous form of moral rearmament. We seem to have had nothing to say to the defeated unless they could somehow win; no message for the defenseless unless they could manage to put up their dukes. The trouble is, indeed, themselves. That is the meaning of original sin. But the answer to original sin is not miraculous deliverance from its consequences. In the end, the only real deliverance is on another level. It lies not in the curing of our symptoms, but in the drawing of our diseases into the mystery of the Passion. What Christianity promises is not the removal of evil from this world, but the taking of this twisted world into the mystery of Christ's suffering, death and resurrection.

The root of the problem is our inveterate tendency to relapse into believing that fallen man can still manage a straight-line solution to his difficulties. Somewhere in Bonhoeffer there is a passage in which he insists that man cannot pursue any good directly in this world, that it will be achieved, if at all, only paradoxically—through the Passion. That is right. Not that there is anything intrinsically wrong with the straight-line approach. It remains our natural mode of operation, but it just won't work in a fallen world. It was what we were made for in Eden, and it is what we are promised in heaven. Adam was meant to be able to say: There is my wife—I choose to love her; there is my God—I choose to serve him. And he was meant to bring it off. He was to have proceeded to the deliberate fulfillment of his nature as successfully as the cat proceeds to the mouse.

But, with the fall, his faculties weaken and grow confused. He loves; but his love is confounded by self-interest and does unlovely things. He serves; but his service dishonors. To be sure, the straight-line approach is still open to him. He can still get his spaghetti from plate to mouth, recover his strength by a nap, be loving to the child he delights in. But it is no longer the triumphant process it was designed to be. His love does as much harm as good, his health is not indefinitely recoverable, and even the spaghetti obeys him only as long as he stays clear of senility, paralysis and death. There is nothing he can do now that he is not imminently in danger of being unable to do at all; there is nothing he can do well that he may not, under slightly different circumstances, do very badly indeed.

Now when Christ came to save this Adam, can it possibly be that He took so little notice of his real condition as to hand him a gospel of self-improvement and miraculous spiritual healing? Can He really have said Sorry, Charlie, to the whole groaning and travailing world? Is it even thinkable that He is going to write off our catastrophe and hand us a metaphysically inconsequential picnic in its place? Of course not. He will, indeed, provide the picnic (no honest Christian can get around the lavish, even slightly vulgar, beneficence of God—heaven may be analogical pie in an analogical sky, but pie in the sky it remains). There can be no quarrel with the happy ending of the divine comedy. But there is every reason to quarrel with our failure to grasp that He saves us *in* and *through* catastrophe, not *out* of it in any straight-line sense. The deliverance of Christ is in His Passion. It is in the Passion that the Incarnate Word of God exercises His Lordship over the broken and dishonored fragments of history, and it is our failure to take that to heart that makes our Gospel sound irrelevant to modern ears.

Man is a mess, and the world at its most perceptive knows it. He may be a nice mess, a warm-hearted, well-intentioned shambles, but he remains intractable. Why, then, are we so reluctant to come out and say flatly that it is precisely the mess that is Christ's real *métier*? We have put crucifixes

on our altars for centuries, but we have too seldom proclaimed the point. It is precisely the impossible, the hor-
rendous, the hopeless, the useless that is the occasion of His
work. He is here to draw our debacle into His and to bring
His passion into ours. He will not save failures with the
proviso that at some stage of the game they must quit
being failures and snap to. He will, Himself the great
failure, save them *in* failure, *by* failure. He will never tell
Charlie that the years amid thorns and thistles are a waste,
suitable only for regret and speedy replacement. He does
not, in short, tell Adam that his life so far is irrelevant. His
yoke is easier than that, and His burden lighter. Adam has
only to come as he is. It is to his condition that Christ has
stooped; he has only to endure to the end to be saved. And
what does the enduring involve? Only an offering of his
passion to Christ, only an invitation of Christ's Passion
into his. No doubt, Adam will fail in that as he fails in all
else; no doubt, he will do it by fits and starts as he does
everything; but provided he does it at all—provided (dare
we say it? . . . Mercy Himself constrains us.) provided
he does it even once, provided only perhaps that someone
else does it *for* him—the God who creates in failure comes
with power. After that, who is to judge by appearances?

Admittedly, it must be *done*. The mystery by which
the Passion rules history does not operate without man. It
is part of the crassness of the Incarnation: *Man* remains the
agent of history: God reigns over the world, but he reigns
through the *human* Body of Christ. Christianity preaches
no mystique of suffering, no spiritual equation of miseries,
but the drawing of the sons of Adam into the sacred hu-

manity of Christ through the acts of their own history. True enough, the rewards of the laborers in the vineyard bore no relation to the size of their efforts—that is the mystery of the free grace of the Passion; but only those who *worked* were rewarded—and that is the mystery of human agency. It takes both sides of the paradox to do history justice. Yet, when all is said and done, what the world most needs from the church is not so much instruction about the nature of the mystery as a glimpse of the Mystery itself operative in us. It already knows its own passion, and the vastness of the shipwreck of history; it waits for us to show it the power of Christ's Passion and to lift man's agony into His.

Adam and Jesus, you see—history's agent and history's Lord—have been in the same room all along. What a pity we have so often failed to introduce them.